The Top Performer's
Field
Guide

Catalysts for
Leaders,
Superstars and
All Who Aspire
To Be

Jeff D. Standridge

Fitting Words
105 Hazel Path
Hendersonville, Tennessee 37075
www.fittingwords.net

Copyright © 2018 Jeff D. Standridge

All rights reserved. Excerpt as permitted by US Copyright Act of 1976, no part of this book may be reproduced, distributed, or transmitted without prior written permission from the publisher. This book is presented solely for educational and entertainment purposes. The author and publisher are not offering it as legal, accounting, or other professional services advice. Neither the author nor the publisher shall be held liable or responsible to any person or entity with respect to any loss or incidental or consequential damages caused, or alleged to have been caused, directly or indirectly, by the information or programs contained herein. No warranty may be created or extended by sales representatives or written sales materials. Every company is different and the advice and strategies contained herein may not be suitable for your situation. You should seek the services of a competent professional before beginning any improvement program.

Library of Congress Cataloging-in-Publication Data
Standridge, Jeff D.

ISBN: 978-0-9979136-9-9

Printed in the United States of America

1 2 3 4 5 6 7 8 9 10

Contents

So, You Want to Be a Top Performer, Huh?	7
1. Success Starts at Home	10
2. The Big Picture	13
3. Kakeibo	16
4. Train to Win	19
5. Can I Take a Moment of Your Time?	22
6. Perception Is Reality	25
7. The Royal Flower of Success	28
8. Coffee Is for Closers	31
9. Fear of Success	34
10. Working from Home	37
11. May the Force Be With You	40
12. Pattern Recognition	43
13. Twenty-Three Seconds	46
14. Truth Conquers All	49
15. One Project, Two Classes	52
16. Traditions	55
17. Ruthless Prioritization	58
18. The Tao of 80/20	61
19. Stop Being an Idiot	64
20. Shut Eye	67
21. Lessons from Clippy	70
22. Know Your Audience	73
23. The Power of You	76
24. The Winner Effect	79
25. The Big Sur Bear	82
26. Frame of Reference	85

27. Lie To Me	88
28. Making Good Things Better	91
29. Avocado Toast And Mocha Lattes	94
30. Gut Check	97
31. Really, a Section on Meeting Notes?	100
32. The Speed of Change	103
33. Business With Style	106
34. Moscow Rules	109
35. The Nerd's Crystal Ball	112
36. Pushing Rocks Uphill	115
37. When the Earth Was Flat	118
38. Invisible Walls	121
39. The Devil's Advocate	124
40. Toxic Gold	127
41. Winner, Winner, Chicken Dinner	130
42. Duty-Free Giving	133
43. Instant Gratification	136
44. Unplugged	139
45. Scorpion Venom	142
46. Professional Ghosting	145
47. King Solomon's Ring	148
48. The Value of Exchange	151
49. Clear Your Desks	154
50. Activity Versus Accomplishment	157
51. Batter Up!	160
52. Weights and Measures	163
An Excerpt From Jeff Standridge's *Gold Standard*	166
Mini-catalysts	185
About Dr. Jeff D. Standridge	190
Reader's Guide	192

SO, YOU WANT TO BE A TOP PERFORMER, HUH?

I've been studying top performance among individual contributors and leaders for over three decades. I've studied it academically. I've studied it practically. And, I've studied it across multiple cultures in dozens of countries across five continents. One question that drives me is, "Why is it that so many people can generate sustained top performance, while so many others get spotty results at best?" This question has driven me for my entire career as I have examined top performing individual contributors and top performing leaders across startup companies and small businesses, large organizations, academic institutions, and nonprofits.

The fact of the matter is, sustained top performance has nothing to do with degrees or credentials or education or training. Each of these things plays a part, but none of them alone is a predictor of sustained success or top performance. Sustained top performance comes from a combination of how we consistently THINK, coupled with how we consistently

ACT. Of course, our ability to take certain actions is heavily influenced by our skills, the education and training we receive, and our prior experiences. But it is also heavily influenced by the way we think—how we view ourselves, how we view others, and how we look at the circumstances we face. How we think is a huge determinant of how we act. Our thoughts lead to the creation of certain feelings and emotions. Those emotions, in turn, lead us to behave in certain ways. Those emotion-driven behaviors are what ultimately lead to the results we achieve. In the final analysis, thinking and acting have more to do with top performance than just about any other factors.

In my coaching and consulting practice, I conduct over four hundred individual engagements annually with top performers across all industries and across all sizes of organizations. These top performers represent individual contributors and senior executives within organizations, and also include entrepreneurs, innovators, and change agents. I have come to recognize the similarities in their sustained success. I also recognize the similarities in the strenuous emotional demands they face. The *Top Performer's Field Guide* is designed to address many of those demands by allowing the reader to step away from the fray, take a few moments of respite, and establish a healthy frame of reference.

Look, the last thing you need is more work, right? Because you are a top performer, you already do more work than any three of your colleagues. It's the nature of the beast. People look to you *because* you are successful. They lean on you *because* you get results. This *Top Performer's Field Guide* is not meant to be additional work. It's designed to be a "breather" for you—a breather that results in new, immediately applicable insights. And, if you're not a top performer just yet, this book is meant to launch you on the path to get there.

The best use of the *Top Performer's Field Guide* is to take some time each week to STOP what you're doing and to ENGAGE with one of the chapters. Read the material, reflect on the questions and actions and then go back to work. Over the next day or two, think about those questions and actions. When you are ready, take a few more moments to sit down and do what top performers do—answer the questions, plan the necessary activities, and then TAKE ACTION! I guarantee you'll be glad you did.

When you're ready, I'd love to hear about the impact. Give me a shout. It would be an honor to speak with you.

Jeff

Jeff@JeffStandridge.com

SUCCESS STARTS AT HOME

"To be happy at home is the ultimate result of all ambition."
Samuel Johnson

It's Monday morning, and you're chomping at the bit to get your week going. You're looking at your weekly calendar and downing a cup of joe before heading into the office when you hear it. The whooshing, splashity hiss emanating from your laundry room sounds like the *Titanic*'s hull has just been breached. You take a quick look, and the blessed water heater has sprung a leak. There's enough water on the floor to fill a kiddie pool. Thanks, Monday, you've just hijacked a carefully planned week.

Every office has someone that's constantly on the phone dealing with household issues. Is that drama monarch a top performer? I'd wager not. Nothing throws a rock in the punch bowl like problems at home. A chaotic household always spills into your professional world limiting the energy you can expend at work. Then you'll spend your time at home catching up on work, which means household issues go unchecked. This vicious cycle will continue until you reroute the loop. You CAN reroute the loop!

Start by utilizing your professional abilities at home. Catalog your home assets like a project manager would by evaluating each piece of equipment's usable life, scheduling a time for replacements or periodic maintenance, and sticking to the timetable. Set boundaries with those acquaintances who always seem to call you at the wrong times for advice. Create a family calendar so you can plan around school or interpersonal events. Whatever your positive action steps are, the goal should be to clear away personal detractors while at work. You owe it to your employer (or your business), and you owe it to your career to leave your personal distractions at the door. When you've taken care of that, it's time to storm the castle!

SUCCESS STARTS AT HOME
ACCELERATORS

⚡ What personal distractions tend to get in the way of your work?

⚡ What steps can you take to anticipate and manage those distractions outside of work hours?

⚡ What are some of your biggest time wasters at work, and how can you better manage those?

THE BIG PICTURE

"Definiteness of purpose is the starting point of all achievement."

Napoleon Hill

Marine Corps General Joséph Dunford knows how to achieve mission goals. From the Persian Gulf War to the war on terror in Iraq and Afghanistan, Dunford has led thousands of Marines into battle. Currently, General Dunford is the chairman of the Joint Chiefs of Staff and responsible for two million members of the military. Considering the average number of employees in a Fortune 500 company is 52,810, Dunford's leadership reach is staggering. How does he manage to scale his leadership to these levels and still achieve mission goals?

Clarity of intent is the starting point for General Dunford's leadership style. While speaking at the *Wall Street Journal*'s CEO Council, Dunford stressed the importance of everyone within an organization, not just those in a leadership capacity, having a firm grasp of the mission at hand. From privates to generals, Dunford believes everyone must be able to answer the following questions:

> Why am I here? How does this fit into the broader picture? How do my individual responsibilities on a day-to-day basis contribute to that broader vision?

Team members' ability to place themselves within this context is key. Explaining how individual responsibilities contribute to the mission of the organization rests on continually clear communications from top leaders.

The transformative effects of a mission-driven team mean the difference in having problem solvers and problem identifiers. Anyone can walk into any business and, within a few days, identify problems. When we understand the operation and have a personal stake in the venture's success, problems get solved. Imagine every member of your team with that sense of mission. What couldn't be achieved?

THE BIG PICTURE
ACCELERATORS

⚡ What's the mission of your team? Of your organization?

⚡ How can you state that mission in a clear, succinct way that is both understandable and actionable?

⚡ What steps can you take now to ensure your teams identify with the broader mission?

KAKEIBO

"Time is, time was, but time shall be no more."

James Joyce

In many Japanese homes, you can find a simple notebook. Likely dog-eared from use, the notebook is always easily accessible, not far from anyone's reach. Pulling back the notebook's cover would reveal a neatly kept household accounting journal. At the head of each month, there is a record of one's income subtracted by fixed expenses. That subtotal has a deduction for one's savings goal. The final set of entries are a handwritten ledger of every yen that has been spent during the month. At the end of the month, one's spending is compared to the savings goal, and an evaluation of the resulting financial performance is conducted. The budgeting system is known as *kakeibo*. It was introduced in Japan over a hundred years ago, and even the digital age has not yet transformed the process into a smartphone app.

The theory is that when one takes the time to write down spending and evaluate those patterns, financial performance becomes part of a habitual, daily mind-set. As brilliantly simplistic as the system is for finances, the same principles can be applied to any management of resources. What would you discover about your time management skills if you applied the *kakeibo* system for one week? Your income would be replaced with the 10,080 minutes in a week. Our time overhead would be measured as sleeping at least a healthy seven hours a night. Work and leisure activities would be logged as spending money, just like in the *kakeibo* system. At the end of the week, an honest review of how you spent your time would shed a bright light on your inefficiencies. This process is something that I often coach executives and sales persons to complete. It truly is enlightening.

If your first thought was, "I don't have time for that," you're likely already mismanaging your time. If we don't have the time to evaluate how we spend our time, what do we have time for?

KAKEIBO
ACCELERATORS

⚡ For the next week (preferably two), keep a record of how you spend your time … in fifteen-minute increments. (Stop complaining, just imagine you're an attorney and you're billing for those fifteen-minute increments.)

⚡ At the end of the process, categorize your time into the major, similar categories and tally the hours and percent of the total for each category.

⚡ Assess whether the way you're spending your time matches your performance priorities.

TRAIN TO WIN

> "The more you sweat in training, the less you bleed in combat."
>
> Navy SEAL adage

Any discussion of performance is bound to dredge up sports analogies, but the connection between excellence in business and athletics is more tangible than you might first think. The meld of mind and body is unquestioned in the sports arena, but we often discount this bond when discussing business performance. Why should that be on our radar? Unless we're sprinting to catch a connecting flight, there are not many occasions your 100-yard dash time matters in the daily grind of the nine to five (Wait, who works nine to five anyway? That's a subject for another chapter.)

A 2007 University of Georgia study found a positive link between fitness and traits associated with success. Better focus, better follow-through, and higher levels of confidence were all attributed to either starting or increasing one's physical fitness regimen. The benefits of diet and exercise shouldn't come as a surprise to anyone who has had a checkup in the last thirty years. What is surprising is that more professionals don't follow up on this advice.

A component of reaching the pinnacle of one's profession is to secure advantages. Communications, decision-making, process flow are all areas we twist and tweak for optimal performance in order to secure our business an advantage. So why do we not take the time to give ourselves the advantages physical fitness can bestow? It's hard. I don't know how. I'll look foolish. We accept those same excuses for fitness that we would never accept in a business setting. If we accept those justifications in lieu of pursuing the activities that will certainly improve our health and longevity, we will eventually accept those same excuses in our professional life.

Top performance is about a lifestyle of success, not just wins in the boardroom. The quicker you understand that the quicker you'll be on your way to securing whatever brass ring you have in mind.

TRAIN TO WIN
ACCELERATORS

⚡ On a scale of one to ten (with one being undesirable and ten being highly desirable), how would you rate your current level of physical fitness?

⚡ List three areas (weight, strength, endurance, toughness, etc.) relative to your physical condition that you'd like to improve.

⚡ Make a plan to improve in ONE of those areas over the next thirty days.

CAN I TAKE A MOMENT OF YOUR TIME?

"Until we can manage time, we can manage nothing else."

Peter Drucker

It's been one of those days … and you know with supernatural precision how many straws are resting on your camel's back. With equal confidence, you estimate that one more straw will be THE spine-crushing limit. Coffee is possibly the only substance that will fortify your spirits, and you make a mad dash to the breakroom when you hear someone ask, "Can I take a moment of your time?" You break a lifetime of courtesy training and workplace team building by replying, "No, you may not."

If you thought the reply was rude, consider if that person asked you to fork over your wallet. We often say that time is our most valuable asset, so it should be easier to give up your debit card than five minutes of your time. However, we would fight tooth and nail for a few dollars but are routinely complicit to time banditry. The difference between our wallet and our watch is where we place value and our perception of self-worth.

Can I take a moment of your time? No, but I can ***give*** you a moment of my time. The difference between the request and your response is one of self-controlled <u>choice</u>. Anyone who *takes* your time is baring you from achieving your goals and aspirations. Whether through complete altruism or by gaining something in return, when we consciously *give* of our time, we retain control of that precious commodity. While that may sound like a game of semantics, it is a game with a purpose. At the end of the day, time is all we have. How we manage that time often means the difference between success and failure. Top performers maniacally manage their time.

CAN I TAKE A MOMENT OF YOUR TIME?
ACCELERATORS

⚡ Identify your two biggest time wasters.

⚡ Now list out the impact these two time wasters have on your productivity.

⚡ What actions are you willing to take in order to better control these time wasters so you can be more productive?

PERCEPTION IS REALITY

"Leadership is the capacity to translate vision into reality."
Warren Bennis

Without getting into Zen concepts like, "what is the sound of one hand clapping" a person's worldview is their truth. Regardless if that conclusion is factually accurate or not, conclusions sometimes cannot be shaken. You've likely come across this concept in the form of "perception is reality" as it relates to marketing or branding. What if we applied the same techniques to ourselves? Could we believe ourselves into a new reality? Using a technique called guided mental imagery, thoughts can lead to positive change.

Mental imaging is like getting lost in a good novel. With no more than words on a page, you're standing beside the heroine who just saved the world from a nuclear-powered zombie invasion from Neptune. By guiding yourself through that same level of imagery, you can see yourself achieving obtainable goals. Using the classic review question, Where do you see yourself in five years? build a mental palace of achievements necessary to get there. See yourself nailing projects and shaking hands with those congratulating you for promotions. Use the mental war room to anticipate and eliminate barriers to achieving your end goal. Periodically, affirm the milestones you achieve with success-oriented language that extols how happy or fulfilled you are at the different waypoints.

Guided mental imagery also stimulates the same neural pathways as actually performing an action. If your goal is the perfect golf swing, imagining the motion stimulates the same areas of the brain that performing the action does. In other words, your body doesn't know the difference between ACTUALLY performing an action and the guided mental imagery of that same action. When you practice your golf swing, your brain has a bit of prewiring and achieving a consistent swing will be easier. In fact, Tiger Woods was once quoted as saying that he performs every golf shot at least twice—once or more in his mind and once on the course. If you can see it and believe it, most anything is possible.

PERCEPTION IS REALITY
ACCELERATORS

⚡ Search on the topic of guided mental imagery and take a few moments to read a little more about it.

⚡ Now, identify something that you want to improve in your personal or work life over the course of the next few weeks and create a crystal clear picture of how this particular situation looks in its ideal state.

⚡ Develop the habit of focusing on this mental picture multiple times throughout the day, using some of the techniques you read about in question number one above. Track your results.

THE ROYAL FLOWER OF SUCCESS

"There is no royal flower strewn path to success. And if there is, I have not found it, for whatever success I have attained has been the result of much hard work and many sleepless nights."

Madam C. J. Walker

When Sarah Breedlove was little, her parents probably took her to the banks of the Mississippi and pointed to Vicksburg. She was the first of her family to be born a free woman, and her parents likely told her of General Grant taking the Confederate's last Mississippi River stronghold, four years before Sarah's birth. Those stories would end when Sarah's folks were taken by cholera when she was seven. It was then off to Vicksburg where Sarah worked as a housekeeper. One might think prospects were slim for Sarah. But by the time of her death, Sarah was the wealthiest African American woman in the country with a net worth of eight million in today's dollars.

"I got my start by giving myself a start," Sarah was fond of saying. Plagued with hair loss that likely stemmed from malnutrition and the harsh realities of the Reconstruction, Sarah created a line of hair care products designed for African American women. Years before Mary Kay Ash was born, Sarah trained independent "beauty culturists" to demonstrate and sell her products. Thousands of African-American women had the opportunity to participate in an entrepreneurial venture. Sarah's culturists didn't know her by that name, to them she was Madam C. J. Walker. Madam was an honorific used by women in the French beauty industry, and C. J. Walker was her husband's name. On top of that, the name gave her product line a mystique nothing else on the market contained.

Madam C. J. Walker understood that cultivating her royal flower of success meant more than tending her own garden. She used her fame and fortune to advocate African American rights and liberally donated to institutions and charities. She understood that the greater our success, the greater our responsibility to others. Upon her death, two-thirds of Madam Walker's estate went to organizations that improved the lives of others. Her legacy endures as the rags to riches dream of countless Americans, but more importantly, her legacy provided hope and aid to those who needed it the most.

THE ROYAL FLOWER OF SUCCESS
ACCELERATORS

⚡ Briefly describe where your own path to success has been a bit rocky.

⚡ What actions did you take to successfully traverse that rocky path?

⚡ What lessons do you have tucked away from that prior experience that might be useful to you in the future?

COFFEE IS FOR CLOSERS

"Let go of the people who dull your shine, poison your spirit and bring you drama. Cancel your subscription to their issues."

Steve Maraboli

I cringe when I think about Alec Baldwin's iconic, "closers get coffee" scene in *Glengarry Glen Ross*. The profanity-laden tirade is the antithesis of servant leadership and exemplifies everything off beam in the American workplace. If you've never seen the clip, find it online, and sit through every smarmy second of it. Why would I ask you to watch a piece of film that is rapacious? Because those seven minutes display a hidden truth.

No matter how much we wish it were not so, the Alec Baldwins do exist in today's workplaces. At some point, you will have to deal with a client, coworker, or leader whose bombastic behavior crashes the boundaries of appropriate workplace conduct. To make matters worse, leaders often cover or make excuses for such characters because they are "rainmakers" or "sales closers." It's not appropriate by any measure, but that is the reality of the world.

Now, I'm no saint for sure. But as one who has studied top performance for over three decades it's impossible to reconcile in my mind how the this type of behavior leads to sustainable results. Why do we strive to do what's right, just, and true when others flaunt their accomplishments with inappropriate behavior? The difference is we understand there is more at stake than our own egos. The Alec Baldwins of the world scorch the ground they tread upon, only to achieve short-term goals. True top performers take time to cultivate the same fields to achieve long-term sustainable results. We have faith that our efforts go beyond the office and transcend into higher realms than bonuses or balance sheets. That faith is our comfort when we stand nose to nose and toes to toes with the Alec Baldwins of the world.

The next time you're told, "coffee is for closers," or some other asinine statement, get your coffee from someone who follows the same path as you.

COFFEE IS FOR CLOSERS
ACCELERATORS

🗲 Find the *Glengarry Glen Ross* clip online and watch it in its entirety.

🗲 Who are the Alec Baldwins of your business or workplace and what are their notorious quips?

🗲 What quips or quotes are you known for that others might perceive as "Alec Baldwin–ish?"

FEAR OF SUCCESS

"Everything you want is on the other side of fear."

Jack Canfield

Spiders, clowns, flying, and enclosed spaces are all fears people will readily admit to. One thing you will never hear someone say is they are afraid to succeed. In consulting, I constantly see actions that scream, "I'm comfortable where I'm at, and I don't need to take the next step." Missed deadlines, multiple unfinished projects, infinite second-guessing, and always missing the brass ring by inches are all red flags you may be afraid to succeed. These behaviors self-sabotage any chance of forward momentum. If you fall into this category, I know your secret. I know you wouldn't be reading this text unless you've recognized the Jekyll and Hyde duking it out in your mind. You want to be the successful Dr. Jekyll, but you don't precisely know why the doubting Mr. Hyde is holding you back.

Here's a dose of truth—you're worth succeeding. Period. There is no "but" to that statement. If you read, "you're worth succeeding," and automatically tacked on a qualifier, there's where Mr. Hyde gets his power. Often these doubts stem from not wanting to be in the spotlight. Promotions, career changes, opening a business, or whatever next step to greatness you desire will put you under a microscope where everyone will see your weaknesses. You'll be outed as a fraud or imposter who has no idea what to do or how to lead. If that's you, you've got to change that pattern of recurring thought right here, right now.

To put those fears behind you, you will have to ask and answer a few difficult questions. Why are you standing in your own way? What does the success you want look like, and what happens when you obtain your goal? Then it's decision time. Will you take the incremental steps to be the success you've always wanted to be? Success is a choice followed by consistent action over time. Make that choice and go for it.

FEAR OF SUCCESS
ACCELERATORS

⚡ What are the top three things you are afraid of?

⚡ How do these fears repeatedly impact your ability to be successful?

⚡ What positive, consistent actions can you begin taking right now that will prove those fears wrong?

WORKING FROM HOME

"Isolation is the sum total of wretchedness to a man."
Thomas Carlyle

A few years ago, working from home was considered a fad. Home offices are becoming a reality for millions of Americans as companies look to trim costs and attract talent. Some statistics put employer savings at an annual $11,000 and a 13 percent increase in productivity per employee when one's office is at home. The attraction of commuting from bedroom to home office is a no-brainer, but is it as easy as it sounds? For someone on the track to top performance, the answer isn't easy at all.

The tips and tricks you will find in articles about working from home rarely address the isolation that stems from a home office. One commonly held trait in top performers is the need to socialize. We thrive in collaborative environments and draw strength from the energy interpersonal contact generates. Locking yourself away in a home office cuts off an important element that elevates our game beyond our peers. No matter how many video conferences or phone calls we make in a day, there's no replacing human contact.

Top performance is never an all about you proposition. Top performance is a people proposition. The danger of staying chained to your desk is turning your career into a version of Jack Nicholson in *The Shining*. So when you're not feeling connected to the world, get out. Walk around the block, go to your apartment's common area and strike up a conversation, visit a coffee shop, but do something to reinvigorate your prime energy source. Simply being around others for a few minutes should get you back on track to greatness no matter where your office is located.

WORKING FROM HOME
ACCELERATORS

⚡ Take some time to visit multiple cafes and coffee shops over the next few weeks and try working at each for an hour or so.

⚡ Identify your top two or three favorites.

⚡ Schedule some time each week to work from one or more of these new "offices."

MAY THE FORCE BE WITH YOU

"Do. Or do not. There is no try."

Yoda

The Force was not with George Lucas when he pitched *Star Wars* to Universal Studios and United Artists. The executives at both studios thought the market wouldn't support such an expensive science fiction film and politely shuttled Lucas out the door. Hoping the third time would be the charm, Lucas pitched Twentieth Century Fox and got their acceptance by the skin of his teeth. Lucas didn't receive the budget he needed to bring his full vision to the screen, but he'd make due with what he had. He had originally written Luke Skywalker's home planet as a jungle, but filming in the Tunisian desert was cheaper, so Lucas adapted the script.

Due to the worst rainstorm in Tunisian history, filming got off to a less-than-auspicious start. Many of the set pieces and props were damaged or destroyed. If that wasn't bad enough, the crew and actors weren't even behind *Star Wars*.

Harrison Ford thought Princess Leia's hairdo was ridiculous and Chewbacca looked like a giant in a monkey suit. The man inside R2-D2, Kenny Baker, foresaw the movie flopping as did the rest of the crew. To top off Lucas's problems, most of the required special effects for the movie didn't exist and had to be invented. Production schedules waned, actual expenses burst through the budget's seams, and George Lucas flirted with hypertension and depression.

At the end of the day, the innovation and determination of George Lucas won the day, and so it is with you! Knowing the backstory of Lucas's tribulations to get *Star Wars* into theaters, we hear the words of Yoda in *The Empire Strikes Back*. "Do. Or do not. There is no try."

MAY THE FORCE BE WITH YOU
ACCELERATORS

⚡ What major obstacles are facing your business, project, or workplace right now?

⚡ What things have you "tried" in order to overcome them? What has worked and what has not?

⚡ How can you emulate the innovation and determination of George Lucas to win the day?

PATTERN RECOGNITION

"Mathematics is the science of patterns, and nature exploits just about every pattern that there is."

Ian Stewart

Make better decisions. Seeing that on a to-do list will ruin anyone's day. Every leader from Moses to Musk has wished they could better prognosticate an outcome or choose the correct path. We'll do everything from putting on six different hats to meticulously analyzing costs/benefits to creating elaborate decision trees in order to ferret out the best course of action, but do those approaches really enable us to make better decisions? Evaluating and improving decision-making is highly subjective, but methods by which we marry pattern recognition with making judgment calls is gaining traction within the business community.

Pattern recognition is a term usually used within computer science where a program identifies input data, like images or numerical data sets, and calculates relationships that exist between the data points. Facial recognition evaluates the unique distance ratios of facial features to a biometric database to produce an identification. There are similar programs that assess stock trends or blood tests to make recommendations based on trend data. Here's the slick part, your brain puts any computer to shame when it comes to pattern recognition. You've probably met a financial analyst who can look at a few spreadsheets and quickly tell you the health of a company. That person learned to see the interconnectivity of cash flow, inventory, accounts receivable, and other factors to form a rapid assessment.

Pattern recognition can be learned, and it even forms the basis of capitalism. Supply and demand; boom and bust; consumption and production all form patterns. The topics and techniques of pattern recognition go beyond this text, but the first step is to look for connections in daily causes and effects. A simple example might be tracking why the last ten deliveries were late to a customer. Does the pattern connect with weather conditions, roadwork, supply chain glitches, loading dock callouts, or any other discernable factor? If you see that pattern, you have the beginnings of a data-driven crystal ball that will improve your decision-making process.

PATTERN RECOGNITION
ACCELERATORS

🗲 What business challenges are you experiencing right now, for which you have some data that you can review?

🗲 What potential patterns do you see in the data that might give you a glimpse into the root cause of the challenges?

🗲 How might you "test" those root causes so you can ultimately get to a workable solution?

TWENTY-THREE SECONDS

"Life can only be understood backwards; but it must be lived forwards."

Søren Kierkegaard

George Eastman had a vision that drove his invention of roll film and the camera to use it. Eastman wanted to reduce the cost and simplify the process of photography to the point everyone could have access to the technology. The vision of cameras being as commonplace as brooms led Eastman's company to market dominance for a hundred years, but twenty-three seconds was all it took to bankrupt Eastman's dreams.

In 1975, it took Steve Sasson twenty-three seconds to record a fuzzy 100-by-100 pixel image from the world's first digital camera. Sasson, who worked for Eastman Kodak, showed off the new tech to company executives the next year. Pictures of the meeting's attendees were taken and displayed on TV screens. After processing what they were being shown, the inevitable questions started. Who wants to see their pictures on a TV? How will this technology cannibalize our present film and camera sales? What does a digital photo album look like? Sasson didn't have the answers to any of those questions then, but he knew in his gut that digital photography would be huge.

Kodak poked digital photography with a stick for the next two decades. The company would never fully embrace the technology and went bankrupt in 2012, largely because of this continuing blunder. Kodak's failure did not lie in refusing to embrace the future, but in abandoning Eastman's vision of the past. You see, the entire reason George Eastman founded the company was to put photography in the hands of everyone. Digital cameras represented an evolutionary step in that direction, but most everyone at Kodak forgot that was their mission.

When we do not constantly realign our actions with our purpose, there can never be lasting success. Most mission statements take far less than twenty-three seconds to read, and the example of Kodak represents that review time is well spent.

TWENTY-THREE SECONDS
ACCELERATORS

⚡ What is the mission of your organization? (Don't simply recount the published mission statement. Actually DESCRIBE your mission.)

⚡ Does your REAL mission match your currently published mission statement? If not, correct it.

⚡ Can every single employee describe the REAL mission of your company? Can they describe how their work contributes to the mission? If not, you're missing a great opportunity.

TRUTH CONQUERS ALL

"Opinion is a flitting thing, but truth outlasts the sun."
Emily Dickinson

One night the three bodyguards of King Darius were standing post when one had a novel idea to pass the time. One guard proposed that each bodyguard would write down what the strongest thing on earth was and give it to the king. Darius would be so dazzled by the winner's wisdom that riches and titles would surely follow. The guards slipped their answers in the king's bedchamber, and the next morning Darius summoned the guards to elaborate on their solutions to the riddle.

The first guard said wine was the strongest because it makes men weak and a fortune can be spent on chasing flagons. The second's answer was the king, for he rules and makes laws that all must follow. The third guard countered his predecessors by quipping that women are stronger than either wine or the king. Women give birth to kings and cultivate the vineyards where wine is produced. There was a caveat to the third guard's statement—truth conquers all. For their strengths, wine, kings, and women can all be unrighteous. However, the truth that God will judge us for our actions makes everything else insignificant.

The story is taken from the Old Testament Apocrypha book of Esdras, and the third guard was Zerubbabel. He would go on to build the second temple after the Babylonian captivity. The lessons to the story are boundless. Humble beginnings are not indicative of future greatness. The trappings of the world can distract everyone from their goals. All things should be done with integrity because we are accountable to one who's mightier than bosses or shareholders. No matter how fat our checkbook or ostentatious our office, acting on truth will always make one a success.

TRUTH CONQUERS ALL
ACCELERATORS

⚡ In what ways do you have a tendency to skirt the truth?

⚡ In what situations does your work, your project, or your workplace reward you for being less than completely truthful?

⚡ In what ways can you recommit to speaking truth in all situations, inside and outside of your work?

ONE PROJECT, TWO CLASSES

"Alone we can do so little; together we can do so much"

Helen Keller

When Barbara looked at her phone's screen, she saw a text message she never thought she would see, "Mom, I'm being called to the principal's office, and it's not good." After rushing to the school, Barbara saw her daughter in tears and was informed that she had been caught cheating on two assignments. The principal went on to explain she had turned the same paper in for her English and history classes. Confused, Barbara further probed and found that the work filled the requirements for both classes and the essay had not been plagiarized. There was nothing in the classes' instructions or school honor code that forbade turning in the same work for two different classes. The principal countered that two distinctive assignments required unique work and Barbara's daughter had manipulated the system to get out of doing two papers.

In a collaborative business environment, we often assume the principal's mind-set. Somehow using a team member's work product for our own ends means we're cheating. There's never a need to reinvent a pivot table or write a new report when the work had been previously completed. Individual achievements don't matter a whit if your team falters. Hoarding your work product from the team can be extremely damaging by wasting time and resources through duplicative effort. As leaders, we should praise efficiencies rather than viewing true collaboration as skating by on someone else's work.

By the way, Barbara was a top performing business executive. After a vigorous discussion with the principal, her daughter was sent on her way without further repercussions.

ONE PROJECT, TWO CLASSES
ACCELERATORS

⚡ Where does your project, business, or workplace need more efficiencies?

⚡ What work products already exist that can be leveraged or repurposed to solve other issues?

⚡ Where might you encourage greater collaboration and sharing of work in order to make the entire team more efficient or effective?

TRADITIONS

"People like you to be something, preferably what they are."
John Steinbeck

José came back from lunch completely stoked. The young engineer had been hired straight out of college into a small firm that embraced innovation. One of the company's principals, Mike, told José during his interview the firm looked for recent grads who could inject fresh ideas into their processes. Six months into the job, José saw that Mike had been true to his word. Mike often came to José asking his thoughts on work processes and design tools to keep his perspective fresh. With these experiences in mind, José didn't stop by his cube before running up to Mike to describe his lunchtime discovery.

On one of his news feeds, José had seen an article describing the HR initiatives Reed Hastings at Netflix had implemented. The chief point on José's mind was the "take time off when you need it" policy. The usually receptive Mike soured at José's suggestion the firm implement a similar policy. Crestfallen,

José went back to his cube. Another one of the firm's principals had heard Mike and José's exchange and asked Mike why he had shut down the young engineer's thoughts. Mike launched into a litany of reasons ranging from the disparity between their small shop and the talent pool of Netflix, but the final emphatic point was that for the last thirty years he had to schedule vacation time and by Ned, he wasn't going to let a rookie take off on a whim.

Someone like José will be far less likely to present new ideas in any area after an exchange like that. We cannot simply turn an innovative workplace off and on like a light switch. Either we foster an environment that craves new ideas and evaluates them on the basis of their true merits, or we cling to our outmoded biases and work processes. True innovators do not pick and choose what topics are fair game for innovation. Either you're an innovator, or you aren't.

TRADITIONS
ACCELERATORS

🗲 On a scale of one to ten (one being low and ten being high), how would you rate the "spirit of innovation" in your project, business, or workplace?

🗲 Unless your rating was an eight, nine, or ten, what things must be changed to increase that "spirit of innovation" to nine or ten?

🗲 What three actions can YOU take right now to positively impact this situation?

RUTHLESS PRIORITIZATION

"Sometimes our stop-doing list needs to be bigger than our to-do list."

Patti Digh

Fresh out of a department head meeting your head is spinning. This was the rare brainstorming session that set you on fire with ten solid initiatives that would dramatically improve your operations. You fly back to your desk and go back over your meeting notes to start the planning process. Halfway through the list, like a cream pie in the face, you are slapped with the brutal reality. All the ideas are gold and require working with other departments, but all ten initiatives aren't feasible. You might be able to pull off two of the ideas, and you're going to have to cast eight potential diamonds in the trash can.

You've been placed in the unenviable position of saying no. In this situation, no is not a word that crosses our lips. We're the hard chargers who never say die of the business world, so there must be a way, right? No, there's not. There comes a time when possibilities are infinite enough you must make a choice not to do all the good things for your business you can. You must pick the best things for your business. Steve Jobs was faced with this conundrum when he returned to Apple in 1997. At the time, Apple's product offerings were nearing the point of unmanageability. Jobs wanted to focus the company's attention on four products—a portable and desktop product for the consumer and professional markets. To achieve that goal, Steve Jobs had to say a lot of nos. That's what good leaders do. They triage. They prioritize. They say, "no," when saying "yes" would be a lot easier and certainly more palatable.

We must abandon the belief that saying no means giving up. Saying no when prioritizing is a tool, not an excuse. Somewhere in the process there will be wailing and gnashing of teeth, but the prudent use of the word *no* will save greater heartache in the future. And, it just might enable the "yes" that changes the world.

RUTHLESS PRIORITIZATION
ACCELERATORS

⚡ What are all of the potential "yesses" you're being faced with currently?

⚡ How many of those do you really have the resources and bandwidth to tackle right now?

⚡ Which of those projects or initiatives have the greatest potential for positive impact and which ones must you say "no" to, for now?

THE TAO OF 80/20

> "When it is useful to them, men can believe a theory of which they know nothing more than its name."
>
> Vilfredo Pareto

Business speak is rife with fortune cookie adages we believe to be true but are woefully unquantifiable. Henry Ford's, "If you always do what you've always done, you'll always get what you've always got," is great advice, but there's no reasonable way to measure the get versus the got. We love gauged metrics and the 80/20 rule is worthy of examination. Does 20 percent of an organization really do 80 percent of the work, or is that something the workhorses made up to make everyone else step up their game?

The 80/20 rule can be traced back to an 1896 paper by Italian polymath Vilfredo Pareto. His initial claim was that 80 percent of the land in Italy was owned by 20 percent of the population. Pareto expanded his research to other countries and then things got spooky. The distribution of land to population in other countries followed the 80/20 rule. Wealth, as a percentage of GDP, fell into the 80/20 space. On a lark, Pareto found that in his garden 20 percent of his pea pods produced 80 percent of the total peas.

The applications of the 80/20 rule didn't stop with Pareto. What has now become known as the Pareto Principle states that approximately 80 percent of the effects come from 20 percent of the causes. Failure rates of hard drives, word distribution in books, revenue by clients, standardization of stock prices, sizes of sand grains, and thousands of other correlations all roughly adhere to the 80/20 rule. It seems that the 80/20 rule is embedded in the fabric of the universe. What's more, the 80/20 rule is "fractal" (look it up). Meaning, the 80/20 can be applied to 80/20. In other words, 64 percent of the effects come from 4 percent of the causes, or 51 percent of the effects come from 1 percent (actually 0.8 percent) of the causes. Now, THAT is a business maxim I can get behind.

THE TAO OF 80/20
ACCELERATORS

⚡ The Pareto Principle is best used as a principle for prioritization. List all of the things you have to get done within the next week or the next month.

⚡ Identify the 20 percent that will produce 80 percent of the intended results, or the 4 percent that will produce 64 percent of the results, or the 1 percent that will produce 51 percent of the results.

⚡ Reorder your list so that you knock out the 1 percent first, the 4 percent second, the 20 percent third, and the 80 percent last.

STOP BEING AN IDIOT

"Growth is never by mere chance; it is the result of forces working together."

James Cash Penney

Google, Facebook, Disney, and Starbucks ... Sheryl Sandberg has seen her name on the letterhead of all of these enterprises. From a management consultant to the chief operating officer, Sandberg has no doubt received guidance from some of the most innovative business thinkers of our generation, and one piece of advice she received stands apart from the crowd. When offered a vice president slot at Google in 2001, Sandberg was on the fence about accepting the offer. Google was still the new kid on the internet block, and Sandberg wasn't sure which way the wind would blow for the company. To counter Sandberg's hesitation, then Google CEO Eric Schmidt is reported to have said, "Stop being an idiot. All that matters is growth."

In Schmidt's words, Sandberg saw Google and her potential role within the company in a new light. Technology was a growth industry, and that was an attraction, but Sandberg translated Schmidt's admonition to a personal level. The best opportunities are not always with blue chip companies who are set in their ways. Accepting positions, regardless of the company, that allow you to grow perspectives, skills, and confidence is where the real personal value is derived. Taking Schmidt's words to heart has served Sandberg well, and the same message can serve you.

Growing is a decision that takes active participation at this moment. The only growth that happens when we are inactive is to the weeds around you. The longer you wait for the right time or for a peach of an opportunity, the more likely you settle into patterns of doubt and negative inner monologues. The myriad couldas and shouldas become the weeds that eventually choke the desire for growth out of you. All it takes is one step to kickstart your appetite for growth. Reading an article, trying a new recipe, or learning a software package … anything that reminds you that growth is possible do it! Eventually, you'll grow into spaces you never dreamed possible, and it all starts with a decision.

STOP BEING AN IDIOT
ACCELERATORS

⚡ Where have you become stagnate in your personal life, your professional life, or otherwise?

⚡ What's one step you can take right now that will put you on the road to growth?

⚡ Once you take that step and see the benefits, parlay that into the other areas of your life.

SHUT EYE

"Proud people breed sad sorrows for themselves."

Emily Brontë

The brilliantly mad genius of Orson Welles scared the nation into believing martians had invaded the Earth, produced one of the greatest films ever made, and hawked no wine before its time. If *War of the Worlds*, *Citizen Kane*, and cheesy 1970s wine commercials weren't enough, Welles was also a world-class magician. Welles was so talented at prestidigitation, he harbored secret anxiety about magic. Sideshow magicians have long called what Welles feared, shut eye. The term is attached to someone so adept at weaving illusions, the performer begins to believe she or he truly possesses magical powers. It's difficult to believe someone would wake up one morning believing himself or herself to be a spell waving wizard, but there wouldn't be a term for the behavior unless it existed.

Anyone in business has a modicum of the carnival spirit coursing through their veins. We're cheerful for clients and team members when we'd rather go back home and hide under the covers. Doubts are often swept away by a mental shot of "you can do anything" bravado. Those pick-me-ups are a necessary part of our professional existence. The danger comes when we become shut eye to chasing our goals at the expense of our family, friends, or faith. Did Orson Welles really fear in gaining the world he could lose his soul in the bargain? He had racked up more awards and notoriety before he was thirty than most of us will see in a lifetime. It seems more likely Welles's trepidation lay here versus believing he was magical. The fact is, top performers sometimes begin to feel as though they are invincible.

When we become so prideful that our ambitions hold no consequences, the reckoning of a fall is likely just around the bend. The magic lies in moving forward with those who matter to you. Let those people in your life be your touchstone for where ambition ends and an ego-driven success at all costs begins. Open and honest communication and the willingness to be held accountable by your loved ones holds that key. Be sure you guard against the shut eye to that.

SHUT EYE
ACCELERATORS

⚡ In what ways and at what times do you sometimes feel as though you are invincible?

⚡ With whom do you have a loving, accountable relationship that you can leverage to keep you grounded?

⚡ Have an open conversation with that person or people and give them permission to help you keep both feet firmly planted on the ground.

LESSONS FROM CLIPPY

> "Without continual growth and progress, such words as improvement, achievement, and success have no meaning."
> Benjamin Franklin

I've been using Microsoft Word since before the days of Clippy. As annoying as the animated paper clip was, I utilized the feature quite a bit. When Clippy was shelved, it was like the aged workplace sage had retired and his accompanying wisdom was lost to the team. Fast forward a few zillion Word docs and I accidentally discovered that Word has a text-to-speech function. I was in multitasking heaven. The possibilities of listening to a document were already entering future multitasking ideas, but why didn't I know about this already?

I blame my fondness for Clippy. Clippy was always there prodding me to look at this or try that out. Without Clippy, Word was a just another utilitarian word processor. I had forgotten to grow my Word skills because Clippy wasn't there as an infuriating cheerleader. What else had I missed in software that was as permanent a fixture as an old easy chair?

Growth and *change* are words we equate to bright, shiny, and new. We forget that repurposing the old can be more innovative than replacement solutions. From asset management to team members, our first thought shouldn't be "out with the old and in with the new." Our first thought should be, "can what I already have be used for what I need?" When solutions are found within the assets we already hold, there are bound to be cost and time savings.

LESSONS FROM CLIPPY

ACCELERATORS

⚡ Identify one major issue or problem you are facing right now in your business or workplace. Why is it a problem or an issue?

⚡ What simple actions could you take right now, or what skills or capabilities do you have at your disposal, that you could use to rectify or solve this issue or problem?

⚡ Spend the "thinking time" required to do the above and when you're done, identify three more problems and follow the same process.

KNOW YOUR AUDIENCE

> "If your actions inspire others to dream more, learn more, do more and become more, you are a leader."
>
> John Quincy Adams

Pam, an area manager for a big box retail chain, frequently walked stores with her support-team. She liked to get an on the ground view of operations and talk to store associates and customers. During these visits, she preferred to walk alone through the store to make observations without the chatter from others. Her staff took her example and similarly spread throughout the store to check conditions using their own assessment gauges.

While examining a display, Pam heard Larry, a member of her support team, speaking with an associate. As rude as eavesdropping is, Pam wanted to see how Larry interacted with the store staff. She was appalled at what she heard. Their conversation centered on a Mercedes-Benz Larry had recently purchased. He groused about the high cost of maintenance to an associate that made a dollar over minimum wage. Pam politely rounded the corner and sequestered Larry to ask why he felt that was an appropriate topic of discussion. Larry explained that he was trying to motivate the associate to aspire to higher positions and obtain the level of success he held.

While Larry's intentions may have been on target, his methods completely missed the mark. Motivation is a highly individualized process. Everyone has different triggers that ignite their internal drives. While money may motivate one person, a challenge may motivate someone else, and a kind word yet another. Leadership author Ken Blanchard once wrote, "There's nothing so unequal as the equal treatment of unequals." (I'll let you think on that one just a bit.)

What never motivates is a trip down your own egotistical lane. Associates are keenly aware that if you are in a leadership position, your paycheck is bigger than theirs. When in doubt about what motivates someone, ask! Ask associates where they want to go in the company and how you can help them achieve their goals. That is a firm basis for both servant leadership and motivational success.

KNOW YOUR AUDIENCE
ACCELERATORS

⚡ What motivates you to higher levels of achievement?

⚡ What motivates your team members? (if you don't know, ASK and write it down.)

⚡ How can you use what you've learned about your team members' motivational preferences to inspire them to higher levels of performance?

THE POWER OF YOU

"No one ever made a difference by being like everyone else."
P. T. Barnum

There is a subtle misconception that crops up when one reads books like *The Innovator's Field Guide*. When faced with examples of the business community's elite performers there is a tendency to think their methods will spell success for you. We fall into the same reasoning when reading books that outline a specific step-by-step method to achieving your dreams. The authors of those types of books are successful and, by golly, it should work for me too. So, you change your management style or follow the steps only to find you've only succeeded in creating changes that haven't netted the results you hoped for. How can this be? It worked for those individuals, but why are those tactics not working for you?

It could be that there is one critical component to following any example or methodology for success—you. Success comes from what new ideas and exemplars unlock within your unique set of skills and talents, not from being a carbon copy of someone else. Imagine if Jeff Bezos cloned Henry Ford's early philosophy of, "A customer can have a car painted any color he wants as long as it's black"? Amazon would offer a tenth of the items it currently does, and no one would think twice about Bezos's business acumen.

There are authentic, innovative powers inside of you that should never be discounted or even remotely set aside. Are there behaviors and practices that will help you evolve into the success you want to be? Absolutely! There are lessons to be learned and systems to make your path easier. However, pathways to success are as unique as you are. Never forget that you have the power to adapt, evolve, and refine the ideas of others into your vision of success. That's the power of you and don't let anyone ever tell you otherwise.

THE POWER OF YOU
ACCELERATORS

⚡ What key strengths or unique, innovative powers do you possess?

⚡ In what ways do you utilize these powers in your everyday work?

⚡ In what ways could you *better* leverage your uniqueness in pursuit of the key results you're looking to achieve?

THE WINNER EFFECT

> "We hold the keys to victory within us, but usually cannot find them."
>
> John Coates

There's a tingle that starts at the base of my neck and runs up the length of my head when I win at something. I thought the tingle was unique to me, but there is a reason success feels good. Neuroscientists call it "the winner effect." When humans win a contest, our bodies release testosterone which gives us a lift in confidence and a slight euphoria. Losing a competition releases cortisol which has the opposite effect of testosterone and results in sadness and an aversion to risk. The release of these hormones happens, on varying levels, when winning or losing at everything from Candy Land to the Olympics.

Here's the kicker to the winner effect. Long-term exposure to either testosterone or cortisol changes our brain chemistry. Have you ever known anyone that always seems to win? Or, someone who always seems to get the short end of the stick? It turns out that winning and losing streaks aren't just platitudes. Our bodies are built to keep those streaks alive. Imagine this as our bodies giving us positive or negative reinforcement to winning or losing. Research has shown that over the long haul, winners have a greater chance to win and losers are more likely to lose given the trend of those chemicals in one's bloodstream.

If you're at the cortisol end of the spectrum, all is not lost. Remember that winning at *anything* will help reverse cortisol exposure. Competition isn't just measured in terms of you beating someone else. Completing a hike or winning a video game gives one the same hormonal release as winning the World Series. When you're down, complete an activity you know will give you a win. Chain that small achievement with a larger one. Before long, your body's positive reinforcement of sequenced wins will set you on the road to desiring the next success and science says you'll have it.

THE WINNER EFFECT
ACCELERATORS

- Do you routinely experience wins or are you often on the short end of the sick?

- What patterns exist in your most recent wins? Your most recent losses?

- How can you create a "progressive" string of wins in order to take control of your brain chemistry?

THE BIG SUR BEAR

"How others treat me is their path; how I react is mine."

Wayne Dyer

Every summer as a teenager, the future *The Grapes of Wrath* author John Steinbeck would ride his horse up the untamed Santa Lucia Mountains to Big Sur. He worked at Billy Post's ranch tending to the cattle or fixing fences for pocket money for the next school year. One year, halfway to Billy's spread, John's horse cold stopped in the middle of a trail. John nudged the beast with his heel, but not another step would she take. Reaching for his rifle and looking around, John thought his steed had caught a whiff of a mountain lion. Out of the corner of his eye, he saw it—a bear, twice as big as a grizzly and big enough to carry a mule in its jaws.

John's horse bolted back down the mountain, and it was an hour before he reined her in. When he arrived late to the Post ranch, John gave a full account of running into a legendary Big Sur bear. Mr. Post and his other hands crowed at John because the Big Sur bear was a fairy tale and they called him a dirty liar for spinning the yarn. With his integrity questioned, John spent the rest of the summer looking for proof the Big Sur bear existed. He spent his meager wages to buy plaster to make a cast of the giant bear's tracks. As the summer wore on, John and his horse explored the most inaccessible places of Big Sur with no luck. John's horse was injured on one outing, and he spent his remaining wages nursing the animal back to health. Soon the season was over, and John had as much money as he had proof he wasn't a liar.

You might think John Steinbeck was foolish or lied about the Big Sur bear. His willingness to forego a school year's worth of pocket money to prove his integrity says otherwise. Is your integrity worth a year's wages? If not, you could be due for some soul-searching.

THE BIG SUR BEAR
ACCELERATORS

⚡ On a scale of one to ten (one being low and ten being high), how would you rate your integrity—the frequency with which your words are truthful or your words match your deeds.

⚡ If your answer was anything less than ten, where must you make changes in order to close the gap?

⚡ Integrity literally means "whole." Therefore, when one lacks integrity, it literally means they are "broken." How can you finish every day such that you are whole and unbroken?

FRAME OF REFERENCE

> "None of us see the world as it is but as we are, as our frames of reference, or maps, define the territory."
>
> Stephen Covey

Business borrows terms and concepts from many disciplines, but possibly none greater than physics. The underlying science of momentum and line of sight is easy to connect, but frame of reference is harder to noodle. Imagine you're riding in a train traveling at a constant speed. If there was a smooth track and the window blinds were shut, you might not be able to tell the train was moving at all. Someone standing along the tracks would see the train zipping along with the full force of its velocity. If two of the train's passengers were throwing a ball back and forth, to them, the ball would appear to fly straight. Those standing on the tracks would see the ball taking a parabolic course due to the train's forward motion. To say the ball is flying straight and on a curved path simultaneously is a true statement. The difference in perceiving those dual truths is one's relationship to the train—one's frame of reference if you will.

As leaders, we can be blinded by our frame of reference. Imagine you've set a tightly scheduled team goal. One day you see a team member doing absolutely nothing at her desk. She is literally sitting there with her eyes closed and you go ballistic. From within your frame of reference, she's wasting precious time. From her vantage point, she's quietly rehearsing her closing pitch for a client call that is occurring in ten minutes. Without the proper frame of reference, your tirade rattled her enough that the call was suboptimal and now so are your numbers.

Earnestly questioning your frame of reference, or your "mental models," is a critical skill of top performers. If you're prone to act quickly and decisively or to make snap judgments, make sure you understand all the frames of reference before doing something rash.

FRAME OF REFERENCE
ACCELERATORS

◤ How quick are you to form snap judgments?

◤ Recount a time when making a snap judgment or being decisive without all of the facts got you into trouble.

◤ Practice the skill of questioning before you blindly act. Ask questions like, "Why?" "Why not?" "What if?"

LIE TO ME

"False words are not only evil in themselves, but they infect the soul with evil."

Socrates

The difference between success and unfavorable outcomes can rest in the margins. Misreading or being misdirected during a face-to-face conversation can hold dire consequences in any setting. Unless you have been trained by the CIA, everyone has a predisposition to express hidden emotions via physical tells. The nonverbal language is so pervasive within specific cultures, those messages are constantly being coded and decoded when two people have a conversation. Handshakes are the easiest to discern. The weak dead fish handshake denotes trepidation while the aggressive "turn the shake on its side, so the other person's hand is on top" maneuver indicates that person is controlling.

One of the largest problems leaders face is dishonesty. From the little white lies to cover tardiness to larger departures from reality, using body language to spot deceit will serve you well in any capacity. Neuro-Linguistic Programming (NLP) experts suggest that often, liars will subconsciously cover their mouth or throat when speaking, physically attempting to cover the lie before it escapes. Sometimes the act of pointing can be a physical sign of misdirection. If someone closes their eyes for more than one second or blinks excessively, some form of deceit or half-truth could be lurking below the surface. Of course, none of these clues are foolproof. Someone may be blinking excessively because their contact lenses are out of whack. Additionally, cultural differences also can eschew the body language lie detector.

The larger question at hand is, Why does that person feel the need to be dishonest with you? Workplace lies often arise from not wanting to displease a leader or team member. If your reactions to suboptimal results are too harsh, your team may be more inclined to part from the truth. Leaders are lied to every day and will be no matter what your demeanor. Just make sure you're not fostering a workplace where exchanges of honesty carry too high a penalty. Successful leaders and top performers create an environment where truth telling is safe, encouraged, and rewarded.

27

LIE TO ME
ACCELERATORS

⚡ Identify three people within your team you explicitly trust to tell you the truth.

⚡ Ask them for feedback regarding the "climate" for truth telling in your project, business, or workplace.

⚡ If it's solid, ask them for feedback to keep it going. If it's bad, ask about ways to make it better … then do it!

28

MAKING GOOD THINGS BETTER

> "Good is the enemy of great."
>
> Jim Collins

New, *better*, *faster*, *stronger*, and *exciting* are words that are usually coupled with innovation. We want to positively impact our world by showing everyone a spectacular idea that no one else has ever conceived. We want the *Mona Lisa* piloting a fighter jet while sipping a latte of ideas to validate our coveted title as "innovator." That's great, go get 'em, tiger ... but is that what your business needs? Does innovation always have to center around the "we're going to do something new and different" to make an impact on your operations? At some points in a business's lifespan, the organization is sailing along smoothly. During these times, the best innovations might just come from scraping the barnacles off the ship's hull. We need to look at our worst practices that drag down productivity and profitability. Admittedly, examining what our company does lousy isn't flashy, but it can be hugely impactful.

A few years back, a major grocery chain was looking to increase their margins. They had always shipped their 12 pack sodas in low-cut cardboard trays. Someone in logistics realized there was no need to do this. Each of the pallets the logistics center was sending to stores was shrink-wrapped so the cases of soda wouldn't skid off the pallets in transportation. After some testing, the theory held and the cost savings on cardboard alone were hundreds of thousands of dollars, every cent of which dropped straight to the bottom line. That innovation is about as mundane as they get, but the impact was greater than rolling out a new product, with far less risk.

What we want and what our business needs can be two different things. A truly innovative leader assesses the whole business and applies creative flair for problem-solving where the need lies.

MAKING GOOD THINGS BETTER
ACCELERATORS

⚡ Take a walk. Get out and meander around your project, business or workplace. Just walk, and observe, ask questions … and think.

⚡ Each time you do this, go back to your office and take notes on the feedback you receive, on your experiences, your observations, and your ideas.

⚡ After you've done this a few times, identify two or three "improvements" you can make to how the work gets done and share them with your team. Work together to implement them!

AVOCADO TOAST AND MOCHA LATTES

> "If you live like no one else, later, you can live like no one else."
>
> Dave Ramsey

Tim Gurner, a luxury property developer in Melbourne, Australia, made headlines in 2017 by suggesting young people who consistently spent their money on coffee and avocado toast couldn't afford to purchase homes. While Gurner's comments raised the ire of millennials, he's not wrong. Every dollar spent on high-end consumables is one less dollar to invest in tangible assets. Futures are not built on empty Starbucks cups. Those who hold spending habits, as Gurner described, have forgotten that sound financial and business principles should be applied to create personal wealth. The practices of expense minimization, asset allocation, and revenue growth translate equally between home and office.

Many of the 1 percent—the uber-rich—translate these practices in their personal lives. Warren Buffett still lives in the home he bought in 1958. David Cheriton, Stanford professor turned Google stock profit billionaire, cuts his own hair and drives an old VW. Dish Network founder, Charlie Ergen packs a brown bag lunch for work. Aside from being enormously wealthy, these individuals have another common trait. All their parents grew up during the Great Depression and imparted lessons of frugality born out of a life or death level necessity.

More importantly than thrift, the bigger Depression-era example given to these men was that the good times can, and will, come to an end. You might have weathered the financial crisis of 2007–08 and feel like you can survive anything. As bad as that calamity was, the Great Depression was go out and hunt a possum for dinner bad. I guarantee anyone living the high life in 1926 wished they had cut back on their avocado toast intake to prepare for the future.

It's often said to, "expect the best, but plan for the worst." Our personal finances should follow this maxim. Your success will buy you security in lean times and is worth far more than an oil drum of mocha lattes.

AVOCADO TOAST AND MOCHA LATTES
ACCELERATORS

⚡ Take an inventory of your personal financial life. On a scale of one to ten (one being awesome and ten being awful), how would you rate it?

⚡ Where would you like to be, financially, in five years?

⚡ What steps should you begin taking NOW in order to get you one-fifth of the way there over the next twelve months?

GUT CHECK

"A hunch is creativity trying to tell you something."

Frank Capra

Intuitive thought is given a bad rap in a data-driven world. We can't take our peers through a spreadsheet quantifying "that gut feeling" we have about a particular decision point. To say you're relying on intuition feels like an excuse for the unprepared, but your history with gut instinct tells a different story. How many times after taking a test did you look at the results and think, "I knew I should have gone with C"? Your first instinct was to pick one answer, but you over analyzed the choices inevitably picking the wrong one. "I should have gone with my gut," is the near-audible response when you see the red marks on the test.

According to a 2007 study conducted by the University College London, there's something to gut instinct. Participants in the study were asked to identify a rotated symbol in a field of 650 identical symbols. Those that quickly decided which symbols were rotated were more accurate than those who examined the screen closely. The only explanation researchers could postulate was that snap decisions were a result of participants' subconscious pointing to the rotated symbol.

Our brains, after all, perform more functions than we're aware of. Millions of autonomic functions are handled without our conscious knowledge every day. Is it so difficult to believe that the lifetime of stored memories and experiences congeal into a gut instinct without the painstaking conscious decision-making process?

We often exercise the "trust but verify" motto within our business practices, so hold your intuition accountable. Track those times you go against your gut feeling and monitor the outcomes. If the trend leans toward your intuitive decisions being correct, perhaps you should listen to your gut more often.

GUT CHECK
ACCELERATORS

⚡ How trustworthy is your own gut instinct?

⚡ In what types of circumstances are you prone to get strong vibes or gut instincts?

⚡ How can you favor your gut instincts while also holding yourself accountable for quality decision-making?

REALLY, A SECTION ON MEETING NOTES?

"When your heart speaks, take good notes."

Judith Campbell

Taking meeting notes is probably as Business 101 as it gets. Yes, I take notes during meetings ... let's skip this chapter. Not so fast grasshopper. Yeah, you take notes, but are you taking the right notes? Yes, I note deadlines, contact information, blah, blah, blah. Did you note that your client's son has a piano recital next Thursday? Was there a sticky note about the administrative assistant's favorite pastry? If those aren't part of your note-taking skills, you might want to read on.

It's no secret that small personal connections with clients can make the difference between just pounding the pavement and bringing home the deal. Calling your client Friday morning to see how little Johnny's piano recital went or bringing a piece of baklava the next time you're in the office could go a long way toward sealing the deal … toward securing someone's business. If price, service, and quality are equal, who are you most likely to place an order with? The person who sent you a handpicked and signed birthday card, or the person who only calls to see if you've run out of widgets?

Making client, or even team member, connections on this level gives an added value to the relationship experience. As you probably deal with hundreds of people a week, keep a short list of personal follow-up items as part of your meeting prep. This is not meant to be a creepy, stalkerish list of inappropriate information. With the sheer number of contacts you likely have, a reminder mechanism of this value-added proposition is necessary. Over time, as you build strong, trust-based relationships with your prospects, clients, and colleagues, the need for these types of memory joggers will wane. Until it does, these notes could mean the difference between "so-so" and being stellar!

REALLY, A SECTION ON MEETING NOTES? *ACCELERATORS*

⚡ Name your top three clients and your top two internal stakeholders.

⚡ Now, write down three important facts or "nuances" you know about each one of them … things that are important to THEM.

⚡ Now, list your top ten external clients and your top ten internal stakeholders. Make it your mission to learn what's important to them.

THE SPEED OF CHANGE

> "Even those who fancy themselves the most progressive will fight against other kinds of progress, for each of us is convinced that our way is the best way."
>
> Louis L'Amour

Amazon's 2017 acquisition of Whole Foods raised eyebrows among business pundits. Jeff Bezos' left field maneuver made sense when examining Amazon's goal of creating return customers based on conveniently delivered consumables. Whole Foods would benefit from Amazon's economy of scale and distribution techniques. Amazon's stock got a shot in the arm, and the headlines faded, but how are those changes going?

Business Insider reported in early 2018 that Whole Foods employees are having difficulties with the velocity of change the association with Amazon is bringing. The point of contention centers around the implementation of centralized purchasing and a unifying inventory control system in Whole Foods stores. The report indicates that Whole Foods had utilized a regional, or in some cases, a store-level acquisition system. Associates ordered products from whichever vendor fit their local markets. Never having dealt with coordinated buying or an amalgamated inventory system, reports are indicating Whole Foods associates are nearing the point of revolt.

No matter the veracity of *Business Insider*'s reporting, it illustrates leaders must gauge their teams' tolerance for change during the planning process. Adaptation is a learned skill that leaders must teach if the winds of change are aloft. Half of that process is in gaining critical buy in by developing clear change goals and in illustrating the benefits of the change initiatives to associates. The second half is regardless of the speed of change, a support network must be in place to facilitate those initiatives. Proclaiming a new inventory system is two weeks out and handing out manuals won't cut it. Like planning the supply and logistics side of any initiative, a people plan for the velocity of change must exist. If that's been overlooked, what could be happening at Whole Foods could be just around the corner for you as well.

THE SPEED OF CHANGE
ACCELERATORS

⚡ What major changes are you attempting to implement within your project, business, or workplace?

⚡ What plans do you have in place to ensure the people responsible for those changes are brought in and ready to implement and sustain them?

⚡ Identify the potential "problem areas" and create a list of key actions required to mitigate those risks.

BUSINESS WITH STYLE

> "I think there is beauty in everything. What 'normal' people would perceive as ugly, I can usually see something of beauty in it."
>
> Alexander McQueen

Few industries are as future-oriented as fashion. Most industries look to product lines in the three to five-year range. Fashion lines literally change with the season. The hunt for the next big thing is not some nebulous forecast of the future. It's the *modus operandi* of the entire fashion world. Traditionally, next year's clothing lines are a best guess based on cultural trends and broad-reaching lifestyle. For example, there has been a concerted effort in the industry to fuse technology with fashion. From wearable technology to smart materials that can change color or texture, fashion always strives to be a cutting-edge synthesis of differing industries.

Julia Fowler took the interdisciplinary approach when she formed EDITED, a fashion trend forecasting company. Fowler decided to take an analytical approach to the creatively intuitive industry. Speaking to the *New York Times*, Fowler said:

> Industries like the financial sector have used big data for many years. The logical step for us was to apply a scientific approach to the apparel industry.

Partnering with a financial model programmer, EDITED created a software platform that analyzes over 300,000 comments on social media daily. EDITED's platform gauges consumer moods based on comments on social media remarks from pricing to style preferences. This data is used to project how the fashion landscape will look in the future.

EDITED embodies the future, and that's not because Fowler created a technological answer to predict fashion trends. The future is about merging different approaches and industries together to create synergy. A future orientation is about opening your mind to dissimilar possibilities and seeing opportunities that no one else visualizes. Are you prepared for that type of mind-set? If you're not, someone else is.

BUSINESS WITH STYLE
ACCELERATORS

✘ What does the ideal future look like for your business, project, or workplace?

✘ What steps or key actions must you take to bring that ideal future to fruition?

✘ What things must you correct or stop doing if your vision is to become reality?

MOSCOW RULES

"There is no place where espionage is not possible."

Sun Tzu

The rivalry between the United States and the Soviet Union during the Cold War was a frightening a time to live. The cloud of nuclear threat hung on the brinksmanship of political leaders and the efforts of intelligence services trying to decipher their opponent's intentions. Cold War American and British spies developed a set of unofficial rules when operating in enemy territory. Known as "Moscow Rules," these guidelines were wisdom bombs for deep cover agents:

> Assume nothing. Never go against your gut. Do not look back; you are never completely alone. Vary your pattern and stay within your cover. Do not harass the opposition. Pick the time and place for action. Keep your options open.

The various business applications of Moscow Rules are plentiful enough to fill a stand-alone book, but "do not look back; you are never completely alone" deserves closer examination. If you're a pessimist, this rule is interpreted as watch what you say and do because you never know who's observing. That's certainly true, but since you are a person of integrity that should never be an issue for you. Spin it just a little, and the positive meaning of this rule is that someone on your team always has your back, so there's no reason to constantly seek that validation.

Another rule that sticks out is, "vary your pattern and stay within your cover." Cover for a spy is the persona they adopt while in the field. Our cover is our mission and business acumen. Varying our pattern means we should always strive for positive change by maintaining a future-oriented outlook. When we seek opportunities to grow our business "within our cover," we can operate in any unknown territory because we operate by a clear set of guiding principles.

Who knew taking lessons from real-world James Bonds could help you succeed?

MOSCOW RULES
ACCELERATORS

🗲 Which of the Moscow Rules seem most applicable to your business, project, or workplace?

🗲 How do those rules regularly play out in your business, project, or workplace today?

🗲 How can you apply the positive aspect of those Moscow Rules going forward?

THE NERD'S CRYSTAL BALL

"Change occurs on a continuum and does not move in a straight line."

Sharon Weil

There was a time when being a nerd was not cool. Parents of precocious children often consoled, "Keep on reading and don't worry about them; they'll work for you one day," even when their child was chided for reading at a pep rally. The digital age proved that reading was infinitely better advice than even finishing your English peas. One of the common traits of successful people is a voracious appetite for the written word. A 2014 study by CNBC contributor Tom Corley, stated that 88 percent of wealthy individuals he interviewed read at least thirty minutes a day. Access to new ideas, current trends, and refreshing skills are all a function of reading. Make no mistake about it, reading and self-study is a key contributor to success.

The advantages of reading go farther through the looking glass when one reads science fiction. Good science fiction writers are unfettered by the shackles of currently available technology, but base their ideas on sound scientific principles. This has created a chicken and egg proposition for real-world technology innovators. How many of the inventions that are commonplace today were inspired by the impossibilities of science fiction? Arthur C. Clarke showcased tablet PCs and virtual reality games in his works of the 1950s and 60s. H. G. Wells envisioned tanks, atomic weapons, and automatic doors near the turn of the last century. Hugo Gernsback pegged radar and video conferencing before the start of World War I.

The prophetic abilities of these, and other, science fiction authors aren't as important, however, as the inspiration they provided. Real-world tech developers have turned what were flights of fancy into workable products by wondering, "how could I make that happen?" The magic of reading is the limitless possibilities the imagination holds and depending on what you read, you might stumble on the next big thing.

THE NERD'S CRYSTAL BALL
ACCELERATORS

⚡ How much time do you spend focused on reading or personal self-study?

⚡ Carve out some time each day or each week (thirty minutes a day is about two and a half hours a week or 5 percent of your average work week) and dedicate it to self-improvement.

⚡ If all else fails to produce the available time, leverage any 'nonproductive' time you have for reading or listening to audiobooks.

PUSHING ROCKS UPHILL

"The foolish man seeks happiness in the distance. The wise grows it under his feet."

James Oppenheim

The Greek mythological figure of Sisyphus is familiar to most of us even if we don't remember his name. He's the poor guy that was doomed by the gods to eternal pointless labor. Each morning, Sisyphus would wake up at the base of a mountain and was tasked with rolling a ginormous rock to the summit. Each day, Sisyphus would perform this duty. Exhausted, Sisyphus would fall asleep at the mountaintop. The next morning, he awakened to a boulder at the bottom of the mountain just to do it all over again.

The plight of Sisyphus has been used in countless texts as a cautionary reference to a pointless work task. There's a different way to look at Sisyphus, however. Albert Camus, the 1957 Nobel laureate for literature, postulated in his 1940 essay,

"The Myth of Sisyphus," that we are looking at Sisyphus from the wrong side up. Camus wrote:

> If the descent [Sisyphus waking up at the bottom of the mountain] is sometimes performed in sorrow, it can also take place in joy. The struggle itself toward the heights is enough to fill a man's heart. One must imagine Sisyphus happy.

Is it possible for Sisyphus to be happy in his labors without the appearance of success?

I would argue that Sisyphus was successful and experienced a daily reward. Every day he was successful in pushing the rock into the highlands. The reward for his labors was reaching a mountaintop with a view that few, if any, had ever seen. When we change our point of view, we can appreciate the summits we've reached no matter how repetitive or doleful the labor might seem. If we don't push a few rocks uphill, there is no chance of seeing anything but the bottom of the mountain.

PUSHING ROCKS UPHILL
ACCELERATORS

⚡ Where do you feel like you're "pushing a rock uphill"? What's the specific circumstance?

⚡ How might you look at that experience differently? What are the positives in that process and what are the negatives?

⚡ Taking that new perspective, focus on making the critical changes to the process while being careful not to remove the positive parts of the process.

WHEN THE EARTH WAS FLAT

"Reality is that which, when you stop believing in it, doesn't go away."

Philip K. Dick

Only one of the following two statements is true. Care to fancy a guess?

A: One of Christopher Columbus's goals in crossing the Atlantic Ocean was to prove the Earth is round.

B: The Earth is a sphere and orbits the Sun.

Unless you're a member of the Flat Earth Society (yes, that's a real organization), you might be having a problem believing statement A is false. As early as the sixth century BC, Pythagoras and Euclid wrote about the Earth being round. Even in the 1200s an astronomy text, called *On the Sphere of the World*, was circulated in universities until the time of Copernicus. The story of Columbus and the flat Earth was presented in a number of 1800s books and has stuck ever since.

If you were conflicted about the veracity of both statements, you've experienced what psychologists call cognitive dissonance. The principle states that humans experience distress when we hold multiple contradictory beliefs, values, or ideas. That conflict may cause us to do or believe things that are uncharacteristic. In down to round Earth terms, cognitive dissonance is one of the reasons we have lapses in judgment and actions. For example, you abhor profanity, but tell an off-color joke to a tight-knit group of bawdy coworkers. You simultaneously believe that profanity is wrong and to be part of the team you must find acceptance from this foul-mouthed group.

When we better understand our own behavior, we can develop strategies to align our beliefs with our actions. Everyone has had the "why did I do or say that … " moment. Use those missteps for instructive introspection rather than regret or self-loathing. When you can discover those blind spots within yourself, you are more likely to see the bigger picture. Misalignment of an organization's mission, vision, and values can be caused by the same cognitive dissonance. That fresh set of eyes will start seeing through the blind spots that are holding you and your venture back from achieving greatness.

WHEN THE EARTH WAS FLAT
ACCELERATORS

⚡ Examine the mission, vision, and values of your organization or workplace. Are they consistent? Do they have meaning? Do they drive positive workplace behavior?

⚡ Where are you prone to have personal "blind spots" in your work and/or in your leadership with others?

⚡ What things can you do now to begin behaving more consistently with your mission, vision, and values?

INVISIBLE WALLS

> "It makes a difference, doesn't it, whether we fence ourselves in, or whether we are fenced out by the barriers of others?"
>
> E. M. Forster

One burden of leadership is that invisible walls can exist between ourselves and our team members. Some of these barriers we can understand and work to limit. We use the sledgehammers of encouragement, professional development, and public recognition to reach through to our team. However, there are some walls that we might not recognize due to organizational policy. As stewards of our respective businesses, we are honor bound to follow the various policies and procedures of the organization. Those very guidelines, however, might be creating walls you never imagined existed.

Imagine your company issues credit cards to the leadership for travel expenses. The practice is common enough for those who frequently travel, and you might take the practice for granted. How does your company handle travel expenses for team members that don't often go in the field? If your company requires those without a credit card to "front" the funds for the travel expenses and then submit for reimbursement later, there could be a wall that's invisible to you. In this reimbursable model, sundry travel expenses come out of your associate's pocket. The associate then must wait the applicable reimbursement period to recoup those funds. That associate has basically loaned the company money. You, on the other hand, have a credit card and not a penny of expenses comes from your personal piggy bank. There's an invisible wall that can cause resentment due to no fault of your own.

The easy path is to let those institutional invisible walls exist by using the standby "that's what they want upstairs, so that's what we've got to work with." If that's your stance when an invisible wall turns bright red in front of your eyes, you're a figurehead and not a leader. Leaders address team concerns up the ladder with tact and decorum. Your team will let you know where those invisible walls exist if you take a moment to listen to them.

INVISIBLE WALLS
ACCELERATORS

🗲 Create a regular and consistent process whereby you meet with all of your team members to hear what's on their mind—no real agenda, other than to ask them a series of open-ended questions about themselves, the workplace, their work, and for feedback about how things are running.

🗲 Take notes to capture important points about the discussion. After meeting with everyone, create a list of "themes" or items that need to be addressed up the chain, down the chain, and across the group.

🗲 Build a plan to drive positive impact in your team and the organization as a result of this gold mine of feedback.

THE DEVIL'S ADVOCATE

> "If it's creativity you're after, ask your employees to solve problems alone before sharing their ideas. If you want the wisdom of the crowd, gather it electronically, or in writing, and make sure people can't see each other's ideas until everyone has had a chance to contribute."
>
> Susan Cain

Flying anywhere in the world during the early days of October 2001 was an exercise in fear and paranoia. The September 11 attacks were not a month gone, and the aviation industry was reeling from the repercussions of the terrorism. Airlines needed time to adjust to the chaos, and a bit of good news wouldn't hurt matters. That was not to be when 39,000 Swissair passengers found themselves stranded at airports throughout the world on October 2. All Swissair flights were canceled, and ticket counters closed. Rumors of another terrorist plot circulated terminals, but Swissair's problems were mundane in comparison. The company had run out of money.

Swissair had a sterling reputation in the aviation community, often being called the Flying Bank for impressive runs of profitability and expansion. Running up to 2000, airline deregulations and increased competition degraded Swissair's financial picture. The situation was so dire that in 2000 alone, Swissair nearly doubled its debt to a whopping $9 billion and was bleeding cash. Swissair's board made cutbacks but was not concerned about the debt—because they were the Flying Bank. The board thought things would turn around and boy, they did. On October 2, 2001, Swissair's debt load was massive enough that no financial institution in the world would loan them another franc. The airline didn't have the funds to pay for fuel or airport taxes, so all operations suddenly halted.

The Swissair crisis was caused by governments, banks, and the Swissair board, believing they were "too big" or "too good" to fail. Each of these entities formed a "mutual admiration society" that made the elephant in the room invisible. The phenomena is called groupthink and exists when no one wants to pose challenges for fear of disrupting harmony. As leaders, we must create an environment where valid disruption is encouraged, even demanded. Ask your team to call you out when they disagree with your points of view. I have been known to tell my senior associates if all you ever say is "yes," or "I agree," then one of us is redundant. Don't be Swissair.

THE DEVIL'S ADVOCATE
ACCELERATORS

⚡ Name three people around you whom you have empowered to challenge your assumptions and to give you critical feedback when it's warranted.

⚡ If you couldn't name three that you have already empowered, identify three that you will empower to challenge you.

⚡ Be overt about your intentions with these three people. Go to them, buy them coffee, tell them you're building an informal "board of advisors" and enlist them for that purpose.

TOXIC GOLD

> "All that is gold does not glitter. Not all those who wander are lost. The old that is strong does not wither, deep roots are not reached by the frost."
>
> J. R. R. Tolkien

In performing research for a prior book, I came across something I never knew about gold. We use gold as a metric to value commodities, ideas, and activities (i.e. "the gold standard"), but gold also has a nasty secret. Gold is commonly found naturally in small quantities and scarcity is a factor in the metal's intrinsic value. There are geological conditions that produce large quantities of gold. Those deposits are sometimes found near volcanic activity. There's a problem with gold that's chucked up from volcanos. Gold bonds with chlorine or cyanide to form toxic compounds. It's ironic that one could literally be poisoned by sitting on a mountain of gold.

God's creation and the lessons it can teach us never cease to amaze me. As deadly as large quantities of gold can be, a bacterium thrives on toxic gold. *Cupriavidus metallidurans* ingests the lethal chemicals found in these gold compounds, and plain untainted gold comes out the other side. *Cupriavidus metallidurans* probably didn't start out loving poisonous hors d'oeuvres, but the bacterium adapted to its environment. If a microorganism can learn how to turn toxins into gold, surely humans in a business environment can do the same. The fact of the matter is, we are the sum total of all of the experiences we have ever had, be they good or be they bad. It's how we *process* those experiences that determines whether we become bitter or better because of them.

Over the next thirty years, business environments are likely to change twice as much as they have in the last thirty years. Quantum innovations, virtual companies, harvesting mistakes, and reverse innovations will become the new normal in the coming years. If you're not familiar with those terms, it's time to brush up on your adaptation skills, or you might be poisoned by the very gold you're trying to find.

TOXIC GOLD
ACCELERATORS

- Identify at least one extremely bad experience that you've had personally that still impacts you today—at home, at school, in the workplace, or etc.

- Why is it that this experience is still negatively impacting you today? These are the "toxins" that you need to properly process.

- Where is the "gold" in these experiences? Mine that gold and use it to put the negativity of this experience behind you for good.

WINNER, WINNER, CHICKEN DINNER

"Leadership is not about your ambition. It is about bringing out the ambitions of your team."

Cheryl Bachelder

Bravado and self-aggrandizement do not inspire Cheryl Bachelder, former CEO of Popeyes Louisiana Kitchen. If you're looking for a quick conversational exit with her, tell her how magnificent you think you are. Bachelder's distaste for the ego of others isn't because she feels her accomplishments outshine anyone else's—although she certainly has the right to feel that way. In the ten years she was Popeyes CEO, the company's stock rose 426 percent. Her business strategy was a straightforward mix of reducing costs, decreasing wait times, and adding new menu items to revitalize the fledgling Popeyes brand. It was her leadership style that made those changes stick.

Popeyes had a multitude of problems when Bachelder took the helm, but her first step was to define what type of leaders the upper echelon of Popeyes wanted to be. The group decided that a servant leadership model where leaders put the people of an enterprise before their own self-interest was the way to go. They then had to decide whom the corporate staff would serve of the company's stakeholders. Popeyes is a franchise-driven business model, and Bachelder saw the franchisees as Popeyes customers at the corporate level. These were the people who had gone into debt or mortgaged their homes to buy into a solid business. Bachelder wanted to give the franchisees more than they had signed up for.

Through national advertising campaigns, addressing franchisees' top seven areas of concern, and an aggressive new menu item schedule, Bachelder's initiatives gave franchisees the working tools for success. Empowering the owner-operators, in turn, generated positive momentum for the other stakeholders of the enterprise. Everything from profits and customer satisfaction to Popeye's stock price soared due to a leader whose goal was to focus on the needs of others—ensuring the success of her key stakeholders.

WINNER, WINNER, CHICKEN DINNER

ACCELERATORS

⚡ Identify your top three stakeholder groups who experience the benefits of your work, project, or business (customers, managers, team members, etc.)

⚡ Create a plan to go and speak to each of those stakeholder groups (individually or in small groups) and start the conversation by asking, "How are things going?"

⚡ Earnestly listen for their feedback, take great notes, and then create a prioritized action plan to actively address their feedback.

DUTY-FREE GIVING

"There are no pockets on a shroud."

Irish Proverb

Charles Feeney didn't want a soul to know what he was up to in 1982. Not even his business partners in Duty Free Shoppers Group (DFS) could be privy to his next move. Trust wasn't an issue. Through the 1960s and 70s, Feeney and his core built an empire of airport tax-free shops dotting the Pacific Rim and the western United States. Feeney was ahead of the curve on business travel to Asia and his chain of shops netted him a $500 million share by 1982. What Feeney was planning on doing with his fortune in 1982 was no one's concern and more to the point, he protected that secret as though his life depended on it.

After two years of meetings with lawyers and specialists in D-day level secrecy, Feeney's plan had gone undetected and he then, made his move. In a few pen strokes, Charles Feeney's ownership in DFS was transferred to Atlantic Philanthropies.

Divesting himself of DFS ownership wasn't a Caribbean island tax dodge, Atlantic Philanthropies was a charitable foundation that would give Feeney's fortune away—all of it. The foundation gave away over four billion dollars over the next twenty-five years and kept Feeney's secret so well he made *Forbes Magazine*'s richest Americans list in 1988. Only when DFS was sold to a French conglomerate in 1997 did Feeney's secret come out, and he allowed his story to be told.

Why would anyone hide that light under a bushel? Feeney never wanted to discourage others from donating to causes Atlantic Philanthropies supported. When the jig was up in 1997, Feeney wanted to be an example of giving while living. Feeney's intent was never to blow his own horn or to solicit or receive accolades. "I set out to work hard, not to get rich," Feeney once said, and he continues to live by his own words. He lived by the adage, "Give more, and you'll live more."

Today, he rents an apartment in San Francisco and lives on less than .5 percent of his previous net worth. Feeney's neighbors probably have no idea they live next to one of America's greatest philanthropists, and I'd wager that suits Feeney just fine.

DUTY-FREE GIVING
ACCELERATORS

⚡ Take a quick inventory of where and how you consistently give your time, your talents, or your treasures.

⚡ The average American gives about 2.5 percent of their annual income to worthy causes. Are you below, at or above average?

⚡ Create your game plan to become a top performer in this area as well.

INSTANT GRATIFICATION

> "A word of encouragement during a failure is worth more than an hour of praise after success."
>
> Unknown

A large part of becoming a top performer is understanding the human psyche in ourselves and in others. The more we can account for instincts that have been part of our genetic makeup since the time of the woolly mammoths, the better we can serve ourselves and our fellow man. One of those primal drives is the need for instant gratification. When the hunter-gatherer within us tells us we're hungry, it's time to go out and hunt. Once the prey was captured, our ancestors ate glutinously until they could eat no more. Who could blame them if their continued existence was directly dependent on their hunting prowess?

Millenia of humans living in agrarian societies nearly stamped the impulse for instant gratification out of our systems. Waiting for crops to come to harvest gives one a tempered perspective on fulfilling our needs. All of that training, however, may have been undone by the digital age. The instantaneous access to information, communication, and purchasing conveys ease of existence that subconsciously translates into "every task should be as easy as ordering a couch online." When our team members are faced with a process that proves difficult or time-consuming, the knee-jerk response is that the task is either impossible broken or beyond their ability.

Leaders have a twofold duty given these circumstances. First, our expectations must be clearly stated with reasonable timeframes. Second, we must fill in the instant gratification gap with timely feedback and encouragement. The hidden benefit of stemming the instant gratification tide is that we are building a relationship with our team members. People follow others they know, like, and trust. The reinforcement that comes from your encouragement will go a long way to achieving those goals.

INSTANT GRATIFICATION
ACCELERATORS

⚡ When was the last time you provided timely feedback and/or encouragement to your team members?

⚡ How prone are you to offer timely support and encouragement to your team members on a regular basis?

⚡ Where do your team members need feedback and/or encouragement right now, and how can you best provide it? Do it now!

44

UNPLUGGED

"Without having seen the Sistine Chapel one can form no appreciable idea of what one man is capable of achieving."
Johann Wolfgang von Goethe

I challenge you to shut down every device around you that is connected to the internet. No phones, laptops, tablets, or talking tech from Amazon or Google shall beep, boop, or chirp. If the thought of doing this hasn't made you throw this book across the room, see how long you can go without turning everything back on. If you made it past six-and-a-half minutes, congratulate yourself. A 2013 study commissioned by Nokia found that smartphone users check their phones at about that frequency. Even if a device did not signal an alert, a different Pew Center study says 67 percent of us will check anyway, just to see if we missed anything.

The point of this exercise isn't to illustrate how addicted we are to digital devices. Being a hard-charging superstar, you feel like you can't unplug because you'll miss something work related. Give it up. Michelangelo periodically put his brush down when painting the Sistine Chapel's ceiling. Laying on his back painting a tiny section of *The Last Judgment*, Michelangelo could not frame the scale and proportion of his efforts. The artist had to stop working, descend the scaffolding, and look up at his work to obtain perspective. You should do the same.

I also have news for you. Whatever your career is, you're not painting the Sistine Chapel. In six hundred years will anyone care about the *work sitting on your desk right now* or the report that was just emailed to you? Likely not. In six hundred years, some far-flung ancestor will benefit by you spending a little more time with your children. You can leave your children with a legacy of love and balance that will be passed down to future generations. If you don't have children, make a positive impact in someone's life. Just do something that makes your corner of the world a better place. Ask yourself, What's my legacy?

You drive your success, but when your success drives you, there's a perspective problem. Come off your scaffolding for a moment and examine what you're working towards. If you don't like the ceiling you've been painting, it's time to readjust your plan.

UNPLUGGED
ACCELERATORS

⚡ Describe the long-term significance of where you spend the vast majority of your time.

⚡ Are you spending enough of your time on things that have lasting significance?

⚡ If not, identify two or three areas where you could have a major, lasting impact … and then pursue them!

45

SCORPION VENOM

"If you dare nothing, then when the day is over, nothing is all you will have gained."

Neil Gaiman

Within the bounds of ethical behavior, you're committed to becoming a financial success. There's no late night, grim project, or problematic client you won't take on to reach your goal. If those statements describe you, I've got a unique opportunity that will advance research in cancer treatments with a $39 million payoff. All you have to do is harvest a gallon of scorpion venom, and you'll be an instant multimillionaire. Due to scientists' use of unique compounds found within the venom and low harvest yield, scorpion venom is the most valuable liquid on the planet.

A portion of anyone's success is the ability to evaluate and manage the risk versus reward equation. Every decision we make in a business setting is a risk. In the spectrum of staying the course to proposing an innovation, there are risk factors along every point. Like a future orientation or culture of change, leaders must be comfortable swimming in the pool of risks.

Let's go back to the scorpion venom proposition and evaluate the risk factors. Of the two thousand-ish species of scorpions, the venom of forty-odd species can kill a human. A gallon of venom will require over 7,500 extractions. The harvest process involves applying an electric shock to the scorpion's stinger, and the venom is mined with a pipette. Using a nonscientific statistical evaluation, there's better than a good chance of being stung by a non-lethal scorpion during the process. Being an awesome leader, I'm sure you've considered using protective gear to limit the risk of getting stung. How does your risk versus reward ratio stand now?

You'll get a gold star if you added innovation to your approach. If you proposed developing a robot that extracts the scorpion venom, you're on the right track. Such a robot currently exists and removes any risk of human contact with the creepy-crawlies. No portion of our skill set exists in a vacuum. Stringing individual skills and prior experiences together creates a synergy that sends our results off the charts!

45

SCORPION VENOM
ACCELERATORS

⚡ List two major issues, problems, or challenges you're facing in your business, project, or workplace right now.

⚡ Outline the primary stakeholders of these issues, problems, or challenges.

⚡ Develop a plan to speak with as many of those stakeholders as possible to get their take on the situation.

PROFESSIONAL GHOSTING

"A great deal of intelligence can be invested in ignorance when the need for illusion is deep."

Saul Bellow

Always be polite and never give away family recipes are two rules ingrained in every southerner's upbringing. From that upbringing, I call a woman "ma'am" and a man "sir," no matter one's age or job title. It's just what I do. That's why I was dismayed when I came across the term *ghosting*. Apparently, the term refers to breaking up with a dating partner by suddenly ceasing communication. Any form of electronic communication goes unanswered and poof—one has disappeared like a ghost.

As rapacious as the practice of ghosting sounds, it goes on in the professional world every day. Remember when a team member sent you an email outlining an outlandishly complex plan to improve efficiency? Remember how that email conveniently found its way to the bottom of the pile for a few weeks?

That's the professional version of ghosting, it and represents ghosting's true face—avoidance. In the case above, you didn't want to hurt the team member's feelings and secretly hoped their plan would be forgotten. It wasn't. That team member will always remember they took the initiative to draft a plan only to be ignored.

In my previous career as a medical flight crewmember, I often heard emergency services workers say they were paid to run towards danger when everyone else ran away. The same is true in business leadership. Our job is to launch headlong into situations no one else wants to tackle. Every time we ghost an email or a phone call, there's a "valid" excuse. I didn't have time. That's on the back burner and can wait. Those are excuses to validate avoidance. That's not polite and certainly not what leaders do.

Turn the situations you avoid into opportunities to create relationships. A polite turndown can be a bridge builder if coached correctly. There's a chance to praise the initiative of the team member's goofy plan and help that person craft a better strategy next time. Turning negatives into positives is what we do as leaders, and there's no chance of that if you put someone in the ghost zone.

PROFESSIONAL GHOSTING
ACCELERATORS

- On a scale of one to ten, (one being infrequently and ten being frequently), how often do you avoid returning emails or phone calls?

- Under what circumstances are you most prone to "ghost" someone?

- What three people do you owe return responses to now? Do it!

47

KING SOLOMON'S RING

"Wisdom is a treasure; the key whereof is never lost."

Edward Counsel

The Bible tells us there was no wiser man than King Solomon, and most days we wish we had a tenth of his gifts. As happens with persons of Solomon's status, legends pop up that are outside scriptural texts. Possibly one of my favorite Solomon tall tales is about a miraculous ring. Solomon called his most trusted advisor and requested he find a certain ring for his king. Before asking any questions, the advisor agreed to find whatever ring Solomon wished for. The advisor then asked why this ring was so special. The king responded, "The ring has the power to make a happy man sad and a sad man happy just by looking at it."

Solomon knew that no ring held that power, but the advisor was a haughty man, and the king wanted to give him an object lesson in humility. A timetable of six months was set for the quest, and Solomon sent the advisor on his way.

The advisor combed through the finest markets Israel had in search of the ring but turned up nothing. The day before the advisor's time limit was up, he dejectedly went through Jerusalem's poorest markets. He asked a grizzled old jewelry merchant if he had ever heard of a ring with the power Solomon described. The aged huckster picked up a plain gold band and engraved something on it before handing it to the king's advisor. The advisor broke out into a grin when he read the inscription and rushed to the palace.

Solomon, seeing the advisor, chuckled asking, if the ring had been found. Without saying a word, the advisor handed the ring to Solomon. The king looked down at the elder merchant's engraving, which said, "this too shall pass." Solomon grew instantly morose. Wisdom, riches, wives, and all the kingly powers he possessed meant nothing, for Solomon would one day pass from this earthly plane just like anyone else.

KING SOLOMON'S RING

ACCELERATORS

⚡ On what circumstances or things do you tend to commonly dwell, to the point of obsession?

⚡ In the grand scheme of things, how important are these circumstances or things?

⚡ Where might you best affix your focus so that the circumstances or things you focus on have a lasting impact?

THE VALUE OF EXCHANGE

> "Money is only a tool. It will take you wherever you wish, but it will not replace you as the driver."
>
> Ayn Rand

Cryptocurrencies were the get-rich-quick buzzword of 2017. The cryptocurrency markets have created fortunes for those early to the party and bankrupted latecomers who gap traded. The market's volatility, driven by pure laissez-faire economics, brought strong statements from traditional financial institutions. The chief arguments against this medium of exchange being that cryptocurrencies are not linked to tangible assets, nor are they linked to the strength of their governments' economies. The value of cryptocurrencies existed only because people assigned a value to a string of computer code.

Recently, I was quoted in a business publication as saying, "Cryptocurrencies scare the heck out of me." Philosophically speaking, I also believe that most absolute naysayers may be a little wide of the mark. You see, value exists in mediums of exchange where we place it. I might not give a plugged nickel for a Jackson Pollock painting, but they commonly fetch millions at auction. Art is different, one may argue. One receives an intangible value for viewing a one of a kind piece of art in one's home. There are plenty of unique velvet Elvis paintings that fit that criterion for less than a C-note, but the value of a Pollock is exponentially greater. The difference lies only in the assessment of quality in both paintings.

Mediums of exchange, from art to cryptocurrency, are hamstrung by a wonky view of value. The world sees a financial advantage in mediums of exchange. Trading anything of value is different for those who rise above the commonplace. We should view every transaction we make as we would a barter of our personal ability. I am giving the best of my ability in exchange for someone else's finest effort. If you've given your all to earn a dollar, would you want to purchase a good or service from someone who has done the same or, from someone who is only doing the minimum to get by?

Only when we begin to view our mediums of exchange from this perspective can we expect the same from our team members. Give your best, and expect the best in return.

THE VALUE OF EXCHANGE
ACCELERATORS

⚡ What do you normally exchange for value on a daily basis in your business, project, or workplace?

⚡ Where are you prone to give less value than you receive in exchange, and how can you correct this imbalance?

⚡ Where are you prone to accept less value than you give in exchange, and how can you correct this imbalance?

CLEAR YOUR DESKS

> "Don't assume, ask. Be kind. Tell the truth. Don't say anything you can't stand behind fully. Have integrity. Tell people how you feel."
>
> Warsan Shire

"It had to be on Friday," thought Sam as he closed his email. A contingent from corporate wanted to stop by Sam's satellite office—on casual Friday. Sam made the rounds informing everyone jeans and T-shirts were to be replaced with business professional attire this particular Friday. Disgruntled moans could be heard in Sam's wake, and he purposefully waited to tell Christy until last. She was the office's cheery glass-half-full person, and Sam liked to end these bad news tours on a positive note. As predicted, Christy took the news in stride saying she had a new outfit she'd wanted to try on and Friday would go swimmingly.

Then Sam saw it sitting on Christy's desk. It was an 80s troll doll holding a gold painted spork. The atrocious thing was part of an interoffice gag, but the sight of it made Sam panic. He'd never met anyone in the visiting corporate group. What would they think of the troll? What would they think of the knickknacks on anyone's desk? No, Sam would not be remembered as the spork troll manager. He ordered everyone to clear their desks of personal items, and said that the only things visible should be work products.

Friday rolled in, and Sam's office was as sterile as an operating room. The corporate visitors got the nickel tour while Sam answered all their questions about operational facts and figures. As Sam walked the delegation out to the parking lot, one of the visitors hung back and introduced himself as the new regional VP of operations. He asked why Sam's office did not participate in casual Friday or allow his team to have personal items on their desks. After Sam's admission that he'd put the shine on for the visit, Sam received the worst dressing down of his adult life by the VP.

What message does it send our team members and superiors when we put on a dog and pony show "for company"? Our team members easily recognize duplicity in our leadership, and those up the ladder are presented a false picture of working conditions. Where's the integrity in that?

49

CLEAR YOUR DESKS
ACCELERATORS

⚡ Be honest with yourself. Are there any areas, at home, with friends, or at work, where your words don't match your actions?

⚡ Where might you have "duplicity" in your leadership practices?

⚡ Where is the biggest culprit and what might you do now to make it right?

ACTIVITY VERSUS ACCOMPLISHMENT

"To accomplish great things, we must dream as well as act."

Anatole France

The mixed-use building was to be the crowning achievement of Smith Properties. This project represented the first time the firm had developed property from the ground up. After securing a prime plot in an up-and-coming neighborhood, Smith Properties demolished the old convenience store that clung to the dirt. The architectural firm the Smith executives picked specialized in trendy mixed-use properties, and their initial renderings for the building were stunning. A modern style fused with art deco would attract high-end residents and businesses. The only thing left to do was secure a few more investors, and within a few months, they would be planning groundbreaking ceremonies.

The partners at Smith decided on a black-tie event to unveil the project to potential investors. The finely crafted guestlist would only be surpassed by the catering and an architectural model of the building. The big night came, and it was time to unveil the model. The mockup had been resting under a satin sheet, and the Smith partners had yet to see it. They wanted a genuine reaction for the media when the model was unveiled. The partnership at Smith properties got a reaction, just not what they had hoped for. The architectural model was a perfect representation of the concept drawings—made of LEGO bricks.

We could hope there's no architectural firm that would make a presentation model out of LEGO bricks, but the story illustrates how effort does not always equal achievement. I'm sure someone "worked really hard" at putting the LEGO model together, but their effort was not focused on the desired result. As a leader, we must be vigilant in where our team places their effort. Had the Smith partners merely taken a peek under that satin sheet, it would have saved their entire project.

ACTIVITY VERSUS ACCOMPLISHMENT
ACCELERATORS

⚡ Over the next couple of weeks, keep track of where you are spending your time. Be willing to be honest with yourself about the activities that consume most of your day.

⚡ Once you do that, compare your activities to the desired accomplishments you are working on. How much time are you spending actually advancing the cause of your goals?

⚡ What changes do you need to make in your activities in order to focus more effort on achieving your desired accomplishments?

BATTER UP!

"You're never too small to dream big."

Seen on a school bus

It was a rare March afternoon that Karen was done with her chores and homework before twilight. She grabbed her softball, bat, and glove before heading to the field behind her house. The season wouldn't start for a few more weeks, but Karen was itching to get the feel of the game back. Choking up on the bat with one hand, Karen called out, "She's at bat!"

With her other hand, she pitched the ball into the air and said, "I am the greatest batter in the world!" The bat and ball failed to connect as Karen took her inaugural swing. As the ball thudded in the soft ground, Karen called out, "Stttrike one!"

Again, she pitched the ball in the air and repeated louder than before, "I AM the greatest batter in the world!" Had you been standing in the field, you would have bet your wallet and watch that Karen connected. The bat passed slightly over the ball, and again the stitched leather hit the ground. In her best umpire impersonation, Karen chirped, "Strike taaa-whooo."

Karen scooped up the ball as quick as a double play and tossed it in the air again. This time her voice reached the Patel's house two doors down as she repeated her mantra, "I AM THE GREATEST batter in the world!"

She meant business with this swing. The bat arched into action again with the full force of Karen's conviction. The bat's wood grain blurred against the background of the budding grass and Karen—missed. It took a few seconds for the ball to come to rest and when it did, Karen the umpire yelled, "Strike three … you're outta there!"

Karen's mother yelled out of the kitchen window dinner was ready a few moments after the third strike was called. Karen gathered her things and headed back across the field. Halfway back to the house, Karen said to herself in an excited voice, "Well whaddya know, I'm the greatest PITCHER in the world."

It's all about your frame of mind …

51

BATTER UP!

ACCELERATORS

⚡ In what areas of your project, business, or workplace do you identify with Karen the batter?

⚡ In what areas should you more appropriately identify with Karen the pitcher?

⚡ How can you apply these new insights in your work going forward?

WEIGHTS AND MEASURES

"A just balance and scales are the Lord's; all the weights in the bag are his work."

Proverbs 16:11

There's no greater symbol for commerce than a balance and scales. The balance and scales have been used to measure both a seller's goods and the customer's payment since ancient times. When a deal was struck for a pound of wool in exchange for an ounce of silver, scales were used to seal both ends of the deal. An honest merchant was judged by the accuracy of his scales, and the same holds true today.

When we purchase a gallon of gas or a pound of ground beef, we seldom consider if the quantity is correct. The readout on the pump says a gallon of gas was transferred from the station's tanks to our car and we go about our business under that assumption. Retailers aren't keen to monkey with their scales because a dedicated government workforce keeps measurements safe for consumers. In most municipalities that watchdog department is called Weights and Measures or the Bureau of Standards. Their field agents test measuring devices and levy stiff penalties if the scales are off kilter. The job is incredibly tedious, but these dedicated individuals keep consumers safe from the unscrupulous.

We as business leaders are the balance and scales for our team. Our integrity is weighed against our decisions. The innovative risks we take are weighed against the outcome of those risks. We weight the performance of our team members against the requirements of the job and/or our expectations as leaders. Personally, we try to balance our careers and home life. The symbolism of a balance and scales is as endless as our imagination, but what is the quality of our scales? Are our scales good enough to receive a passing score from the Office of Weights and Measures? If your scales are purposefully lacking, superstardom will forever be outside your grasp.

Like any other tools, all scales require maintenance. Balancing screws need adjustment, the pans must be kept clean, and the balance weights must be checked against empirical standards. If we are constantly tweaking our scales to obtain the perfect measure, we can do nothing but succeed. Best wishes on your journey to greatness and may God bless your endeavors.

WEIGHTS AND MEASURES
ACCELERATORS

✏ Would you describe your scales as "well-balanced" or "out of whack"?

✏ Describe the rationale for your answer to the question above.

✏ On what things must you focus so that you can maintain the proper balance in your personal and professional life?

AN EXCERPT FROM JEFF STANDRIDGE'S *GOLD STANDARD*

"Leadership is not about a title or a designation. It's about impact, influence, and inspiration. Impact involves getting results, influence is about spreading the passion you have for your work, and you have to inspire teammates and customers."

Robin S. Sharma

Effective Leadership Requires a Delicate Balance

Perhaps you remember the story of Napoleon Hill—the young reporter back in the early 1900s who was commissioned to write a series of success stories on several famous men. Hill credits his success to a fortuitous assignment in 1908 to interview

Andrew Carnegie—one of the richest and most powerful men of that time. During that interview, Carnegie, according to Hill, challenged him to spend the next twenty years studying the most successful men in business, industry, and government and, to distill all that he learned into a "simple success formula" for others to follow. Carnegie himself committed to making the introductions—some five hundred introductions in all.

Years later, in 1937, Hill would publish *Think and Grow Rich,* the book that became the first personal development classic. In it, Hill outlined his thirteen steps to success and for much of the remainder of his life (up until the late 1960s), Hill would travel the country training, speaking, and consulting on "The Science of Personal Achievement."

Decades later, in 1982, Jim Kouzes and Barry Posner embarked on a journey to better understand what characterized great leadership—when leaders performed at their absolute, personal best. After conducting hundreds of interviews, administering thousands of surveys, and examining dozens of case studies, the researchers identified a set of five fundamental practices common to extraordinary leadership achievement. What they learned is that leadership is not simply about having an outgoing personality or an easygoing, open communication style. Leadership is about behavior—how one behaves when leading others, despite differences in age, gender, culture, or socioeconomic status. *The Leadership Challenge,* the book outlining their research, was published in 1987 and has been used by countless organizations and individuals over the past three decades to train existing and aspiring leaders in the "Five Practices of Exemplary Leaders."

Among these "five practices," readers are introduced to the "Ten Commitments of Leadership" which lend substance and meaning to the Five Practices. When stepping back and looking at these practices and commitments from a bit of a different angle, they describe actions that leaders take relative to three specific domains or entities—**self, others,** and **things.** Some of the practices and commitments have to do with the leader him/herself. Practices like challenging a process, taking risks, experimentation, seeking opportunities to learn and grow, among others are specifically related to the leader. While these actions may impact other people, and may slightly overlap the other domains (others and things), for the most part, they are internally directed actions. Inspiring a shared vision, fostering collaboration, and recognizing team accomplishment are very clearly actions taken with other people. And finally, goal setting, assigning critical tasks, achieving small wins are among the practices or commitments that relate specifically to things. At the end of the day, Kouzes and Posner's work has stood the test of time and continues to be used by individuals and organizations all around the world.

A couple of years later, Stephen R. Covey published *The Seven Habits of Highly Effective People*. According to Covey, his research began in the middle seventies by reviewing over two hundred years of "success literature" from numerous writers and thinkers as part of his doctoral studies. Covey describes his process of reviewing all of this success literature and distilling it down into discreet practices that could be modeled by others. He argues adamantly against what he refers to as the "Personality Ethic" so prevalent in leadership and personal development books of the time. Alternatively, Covey promotes what he refers to as the "Character Ethic," in which one aligns him/herself with a set of timeless principles or natural laws.

Much like Kouzes and Posner's leadership practices and commitments, Covey's *Seven Habits* can be easily categorized into habits involving the same three domains of self, others, and things. In fact, Covey himself organizes the habits into those that enable "Private Victory" (self, things), those that generate "Public Victory" (others, things), and the practice that contributes most to "Renewal" (self).

In the early 1990s, heavily influenced by these three works, I embarked on some leadership research of my own. As a young health-care professional, I had the privilege of serving as the president of a statewide professional association at the ripe old age of twenty-six. Barely out of college (I crammed a four-year degree into five-and-a-half years), I was thrust into this position of leadership and readily observed that there were vast differences in how people lead and in how people respond to leadership. I also observed that there were vast differences in the outcomes experienced by these leaders. Some produced consistently positive outcomes while others produced inconsistent results at best. Still others were merely leadership figureheads. Seldom did they produce and even more seldom did they actually lead others to produce. This experience and these observations served to whet my appetite for a deeper understanding of this concept called "leadership."

A few years later, I was appointed to the faculty of an academic health sciences center. I served as a professor in a college that prepared allied health-care professionals (medical technologists, radiologic technologists, genetic counselors, paramedics, respiratory therapists, etc.) for the healthcare workforce. This appointment now gave me the opportunity to study leadership as part of my official responsibilities.

Living in a fairly rural state, our graduates often rapidly ascended the career ladder in hospitals and health care organizations across the state. Soon after graduating from one of our programs, it was quite common for a young professional to quickly assume a supervisory role, become a department director, or even a hospital administrator. The issue was that they had no leadership preparation to do so. In order to address this deficit, I set out to create a course for graduating seniors that would introduce them to the basic concepts of leadership, supervision, team development, performance management, and a host of other baseline leadership responsibilities. It wasn't long before this acquired affinity flourished into a full-blown academic and applied research interest for me.

In the mid-1990s, I began to conduct research into the differentiators of success for the top 1 percent of performers (among health-care professionals), compared to those who make up the middle 50 percent of performers. This research led me into the creation of leadership competency models—observable behaviors that were compiled into specific models that could then be used for hiring, training, coaching, team development, performance management, etc.

Using a research technique developed by the Rand Corporation in the 1950s called the "Delphi" Technique, we created the Respiratory Care Success Model. This model outlined the "differentiating behaviors" of respiratory care practitioners (i.e. respiratory therapists) necessary to lead the profession through a very tumultuous period heading into the twenty-first century. Once again, upon review of this success model, the three domains of self, others, and things stuck out as pivotal.

During the middle of my dissertation research, even well before it was completed, I was commissioned by a senior executive of Acxiom Corporation (ACXM) to replicate my competency model research with IT professionals inside the company. Up until this point, all of the job roles, performance criteria, and other HR systems at the company were predicated on a "skills-based" model, which was particularly problematic during a time when the half-life of all IT knowledge was about fourteen months (or less). Consequently, no sooner could a skill profile for a particular technical job role within the company be created, than it would become obsolete. This phenomenon was wreaking havoc on the HR department of the company. They knew they needed a solution, but they weren't quite sure what that solution might be.

Initially contracting with the company as a consultant, I soon left my professorship to join the ranks of the corporate world full time. I spent the next few years transforming the associate and leadership effectiveness processes and programs of the company from that of rapid obsolescence due to their basis in technical skills, to a robust system based in leadership competency models made up of observable, differentiating behaviors.

During that time, I had the good fortune of coming across Robert E. Kelley's book, *How to be a Star at Work*, and Daniel Goleman's, *Working with Emotional Intelligence.* Kelley outlined the process that he and his team perfected at Bell Labs to discover and validate the differentiators of star performance in the workplace. Once again, the differentiators outlined by Kelley and his team could be organized by their relation to the three specific domains of self, others, and things. Goleman's book, a follow-up to his more science-based work *Emotional Intelligence,* offered very practical guidance for the development of "Personal Competence" (self) and "Social Competence" (others). Golemen offered very detailed applications of emotional intelligence in the workplace and further validated the working hypothesis we had begun developing—that specific observable actions or behaviors across at least three domains (self, others, things) are the differentiators of success between top performers and average performers.

Standing on the shoulders of these giants, we were now equipped to expand our own research process for discovering the differentiating behaviors and building them into replicable competency models. Combining all of the salient points from these four works, we knew that we would be looking for observable, action-oriented behaviors to anchor our models. We felt that the research behind these seminal works was enough to convince us, and our audience, that the true differentiation between excellence and mediocrity, between success and failure, was what people DID … the ACTIONS they took, the BEHAVIORS they demonstrated. So, we set about devising our process to uncover these observable behaviors.

That initiative proved to be both exhilarating and exhausting. For eighteen months, our team worked. We began by surveying all leaders and all nonleaders in the company, asking them to identify the top performers across all locations. Much like Kelley, we also found that there were considerable discrepancies between the people that formal company Leaders identified versus the people that nonleaders identified as the true top performers of the company—a significant finding within itself. However, once we vetted each list of nominees against the others, we were able to declare some fifty individuals, both leaders and nonleaders, as our research group—the universally recognized top performers of the company.

At that point, our job was to identify what actually differentiated these "rock stars" from the remainder of the company population. For the next several months, we engaged each of them in an extensive, recorded, behavioral-event interview in which we asked them the following question: "Tell me about a time at Acxiom when you were challenged beyond belief. You were backed against the wall, staring into the face of failure … but you succeeded." During the course of the interview, we had them tell us about the situation. We had them tell us with whom they were involved. And finally, we had them tell us what they thought, what they felt, what they said, and what they did. The job of the interviewer was to poke, prod, and probe … moving beyond the opinions of these top performers to identify what they actually DID.

During this process, we were fortunate to collect over 120 success stories—actual case studies where these top performers took specific actions that led to success. But once the interviews were over, our job had just begun. The task now at hand involved generating written transcripts of these interviews and conducting a massive qualitative analysis in order to identify the behaviors demonstrated by our research group.

When the job was finished, thirty-four unique and observable behaviors across eight distinct competencies were defined. Dubbed the "Acxiom Eight," these competencies became the foundation of every job role in the company—from the entry-level data analyst to the CEO. And they remained an integral part of the recruitment, selection, training, development, and coaching programs of the company for over fifteen years. But once again, the behaviors that defined superior performance could be categorized into three very distinct domains—self, others, and things. Behaviors involving initiative, results, and achievement orientation or planning and organizing are rooted in the personal domains of "self" and "things". On the other hand, behaviors involving stakeholder orientation, communication or teaming and relationship management clearly require interdependence with "others." And again, in all cases these exemplary behaviors were consistent across all levels of the organization from entery-level to the C-Suite.

The outcome of our own research, combined with the research of those that had gone before us, created an epiphany of sorts that began to solidify a simple yet profound model of personal and interpersonal leadership. This model, when understood and consistently applied, resulted in meaningful and sustained success—whether serving as an individual contributor, a leader of small teams, or a leader of large organizations.

Throughout the next decade and a half, I began applying, adapting, and honing this model with leadership audiences around the world. I was consistently teaching, training, and coaching with the model in the United States; however, I expanded to groups in the United Kingdom, France, Germany, Netherlands, Poland, Spain, and Portugal in 2003–5. From 2005–9, I was able to work with numerous groups of leaders in China, Japan, and Australia. From 2010–13, I had the good fortune of leveraging the model with leadership teams in the Middle East, North Africa, Brazil, and Latin America. Since 2013, I have been subjecting the model to scrutiny again in the

United States with multiple leadership teams from within various companies, institutions, and functions, including sales, operations, nonprofits, education, government, and beyond. In each instance, I was able to refine, adapt, edit and make improvements based on the successes, failures, and feedback of all of those great leaders and groups of functional experts.

What has become clearly obvious, from years of personal experience and observation, validated by multiple researchers, authors, and experts and left unsaid (or at least unclarified) by most, is that sustained individual and leadership success requires a delicate balance between two very specific domains—**Results** and **Relationships**. Effective leaders, as well as effective individual contributors, must maintain a delicate balance between the consistent delivery of results (things) and the consistent and deliberate development of strong relationships with those who help sustain those results (self and others).

This leads us to the *first reality* of Gold Standard Leadership:

> "Effective leadership requires a delicate balance—a balance between results and relationships. Refusal to understand and honor this balance will result in failure."

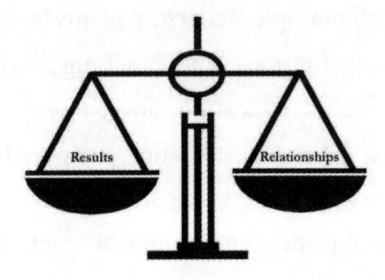

If, for some reason, an individual places an undue focus on one component over the other, suboptimal performance will occur. For instance, if one develops an overreliance on the Results aspect of performance, at the expense of Relationships, she will likely experience wild success, very quickly. That is, until she alienates everyone around her who must help sustain those results (e.g. stakeholders, customers, superiors, team members, etc.)

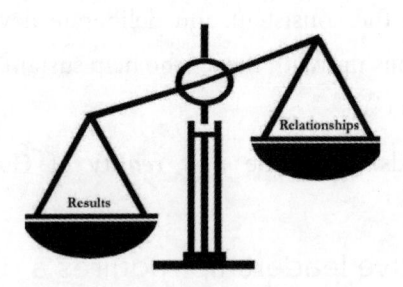

If on the other hand, one places an extreme focus on Relationships, at the expense of Results, he will be very popular. People will love him, until he loses everyone's respect because he cannot do what was promised or fails to deliver consistent results. In both cases, the scale becomes completely out of balance, thus drastically affecting performance.

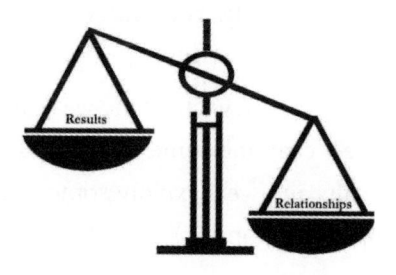

At the end of the day, high performance leadership, as well as high individual performance, requires balance between the ability to manage things and lead people, including the ability to lead oneself. This is where the tie back to all of the prior research comes. All of the prior sources we referenced earlier clearly supported the conclusion that sustained success required a balance across three specific domains—self, others, and things. Our research led to the same conclusion. But after years of validation and refinement, we recognized that sustained performance, whether individual or collective, requires a balance between results and relationships, including a proper relationship with oneself. It is this reality that forms the foundation of Gold Standard Leadership. Gold Standard Leadership is the kind of leadership where high performance—of self and others—is sustained over a long period of time due to the proper balancing of results with relationships. More simply put, it is the form of leadership that produces results day after day after day, while building and maintaining strong, trust-based foundations of influence and relationship along the way.

Throughout the next few chapters, we'll unpack this delicate balance. We'll examine some of the leadership realities that produce results and we'll explore some of the leadership realities that impact relationships.

Reflection and Planning:

On the following pages, describe, in detail, the <u>best</u> form of leadership and the <u>worst</u> form of leadership you've ever experienced personally.

BEST Form of Leadership:

What was the situation?

⚡

⚡

⚡

⚡

What were the behaviors and actions of the leader?

⚡

⚡

⚡

How did his/her behavior or actions impact you?

⚡

⚡

⚡

⚡

How did you respond?

⚡

⚡

⚡

⚡

WORST Form of Leadership:

What was the situation?

⚡

⚡

⚡

⚡

What were the behaviors and actions of the leader?

⚡

⚡

⚡

⚡

How did his/her behavior or actions impact you?

/

/

/

/

How did you respond?

/

/

/

MINI-CATALYSTS

William A. Adams—"When a promise of leadership is neglected or unfulfilled, trust is broken, engagement erodes, and performance suffers."

Marcus Aurelius—"Do not act as if you were going to live ten thousand years. Death hangs over you. While you live, while it is in your power, be good."

Israelmore Ayivor—"The speed at which progress rolls is not determined by the number of people who started pushing it, but by the number of people who are passionate to hold on doing so."

Roy T. Bennett—"Great leaders can see the greatness in others when they can't see it themselves and lead them to their highest potential they don't even know."

Andrew Carnegie—"Think of yourself as on the threshold of unparalleled success. A whole, clear, glorious life lies before you. Achieve! Achieve!"

Bernard Kelvin Clive—"Don't wait for a huge platform before you give of your best performance."

Stephen R. Covey—"I am personally convinced that one person can be a change catalyst, a 'transformer' in any situation, any organization. Such an individual is yeast that can leaven an entire loaf. It requires vision, initiative, patience, respect, persistence, courage, and faith to be a transforming leader."

Frederick Douglass—"I prefer to be true to myself, even at the hazard of incurring the ridicule of others, rather than to be false, and to incur my own abhorrence."

Ralph Waldo Emerson—"Be good to your work, your word, and your friend."

Wesam Fawzi—"The class of your performance is built on the grade of your skills."

Wendel Flanche—"When faced with an exceedingly difficult customer or client, your best revenge is to give outrageous service so you can take their money."

Marcus Garvey—"The ends you serve that are selfish will take you no further than yourself but the ends you serve that are for all, in common, will take you into eternity."

Reverend Theodore Hesburgh—"The very essence of leadership is that you have to have a vision. It's got to be a vision you articulate clearly and forcefully on every occasion. You can't blow an uncertain trumpet."

Napoleon Hill—"Great achievement is usually born of great sacrifice, and is never the result of selfishness."

Ellen Hopkins—"Yes, it takes two to dance. But somebody has to lead."

Spencer Johnson—"Integrity is telling myself the truth. And honesty is telling the truth to other people."

John F. Kennedy—"There are risks and costs to action. But they are far less than the long range risks of comfort and inaction."

Martin Luther King, Jr.—"Every man must decide whether he will walk in the light of creative altruism or in the darkness of destructive selfishness."

Madeleine L'Engle—"We can't take any credit for our talents. It's how we use them that counts."

Craig D. Lounsbrough—"Our roads are most often a tawdry detour we have chosen because the press of pain or the push of greed drove us off the path."

Abraham Lincoln—"No man is good enough to govern another man without that other's consent."

Niccolo Machiavelli—"There is nothing more difficult to take in hand, more perilous to conduct, or more uncertain in its success, than to take the lead in the introduction of a new order of things."

General James "Chaos" Mattis—"Thanks to my reading, I have never been caught flat-footed by any situation, never at a loss for how any problem has been addressed ... It doesn't give me all the answers, but it lights what is often a dark path ahead."

J. P. Morgan—"When you expect things to happen—strangely enough—they do happen."

Richie Norton—"When everyone has a microphone, you can't hear anything. Choose one voice carefully and listen in."

Eunice Parisi-Carew—"People need to feel safe to be who they are—to speak up when they have an idea, or to speak out when they feel something isn't right."

General George S. Patton—"Don't tell people how to do things, tell them what to do and let them surprise you with their results."

Philippians 2:3—"Do nothing from selfish ambition or conceit, but in humility count others more significant than yourself."

General Colin Powell—"The day the soldiers stop bringing you their problems is the day you stopped leading them. They have either lost confidence that you can help them or concluded that you do not care. Either case is a failure of leadership."

Ronald Reagan—"The greatest leader is not necessarily the one who does the greatest things. He is the one that gets the people to do the greatest things."

Beth Revis—"Power isn't control at all—power is strength, and giving that strength to others. A leader isn't someone who forces others to make him stronger; a leader is someone willing to give his strength to others that they may have the strength to stand on their own."

John D. Rockefeller—"Every right implies a responsibility; Every opportunity, an obligation, Every possession, a duty."

Theodore Roosevelt—"The best executive is the one who has sense enough to pick good men to do what he wants done, and self-restraint to keep from meddling with them while they do it."

John Steinbeck—"Ideas are like rabbits. You get a couple and learn how to handle them, and pretty soon you have a dozen."

Sergio Tinoco—"Our first stage of existence is truly honored by the magnificent view of our destination."

Sherry Turkle—"It's too late to leave the future to the futurists."

Booker T. Washington—"If you want to lift yourself up, lift up someone else."

Zig Ziglar—"Honesty and integrity are absolutely essential for success in life—all areas of life. The really good news is that anyone can develop both honesty and integrity."

ABOUT DR. JEFF D. STANDRIDGE

Dr. Jeff Standridge helps organizations and their leaders generate sustained results in the areas of innovation, strategy, profit growth, organizational effectiveness, and leadership. Formerly a vice president for Acxiom Corporation, he has led established and startup business units in North and South America, Europe, Asia, and the Middle East.

Jeff now serves as chief catalyst for the Conductor (www.ARConductor.org), is co-founder of Cadron Capital Partners and Jeff Standridge Innovation Partners, and teaches Entrepreneurial Finance at the University of Central Arkansas (www.UCA.edu).

He has been an invited speaker, trainer, and/or consultant for numerous businesses, organizations, and institutions of higher education around the world. In addition to his executive coaching and custom-tailored consulting, he has received accolades for his world-class presentations, training programs, and workshops, including:

- **Corporate Innovation Accelerator**—for companies of all sizes, across all industries, who want to drive more innovative thinking and problem-solving

Reader's Guide

Topic: Chapter Number

Building Trust: 2, 22, 25, 27, 34, 38, 41, 43, 48

Business Intelligence: 12, 33, 39

Business Tips: 3, 12, 21, 31

Change: 9, 13, 21, 32, 34, 35, 39, 40

Collaboration: 15, 24, 31, 48

Competitors: 28, 39

Creativity: 33, 40, 47

Customer Experience: 31, 34

Decision-making: 20, 32, 37, 45

Diversity: 22, 34, 43, 46

Execution: 6, 11, 15, 48

Employee Retention: 16, 26, 43, 46

Failure: 24, 50

Fear: 6, 9, 30

Goal Setting: 9, 17, 19, 39

Leadership: 2, 8, 19, 26, 28, 35, 38, 40, 43, 45, 48

Mental Clarity: 6, 20, 23, 30, 36, 37, 43, 44, 50, 51

Metrics: 4, 18, 43

Mission: 2, 13, 39, 42, 45, 50

Momentum: 19, 28, 32, 35, 40

Persistence: 1, 7, 36, 47, 51

Performance: 1, 4, 6, 9, 18, 23, 30, 34, 37, 50, 51

Personal Stories 2, 7, 11, 13, 19, 20, 25, 33, 39, 40, 41, 42, 47

Planning: 3, 5, 12, 17, 29, 30, 35

Problem-solving: 12, 14, 15, 25, 47

Process Quality: 10, 15, 17, 24, 32, 38

Success: 1, 4, 7, 9, 20, 23, 24, 34, 44, 45

Team Building: 2, 8, 13, 15, 16, 22, 27, 38, 41, 46, 49

Time Management: 3, 5, 17, 21

Validating Assumptions: 6, 12, 17, 18, 27, 32, 37, 39

Values: 5, 8, 14, 19, 25, 27, 41, 42, 44, 49, 52

Work-Life Balance: 1, 10, 16, 29, 42, 44, 52

- **Faculty Innovation Accelerator**—for academic institutions of all types who are looking to drive more innovative research and problem-solving
- **The Commercialization Accelerator**—for research institutions wanting to create an increased focus on commercializing their research
- **Sales Acceleration Workshop**—for companies that want to build a high-performance sales engine
- **Success Secrets of World-Class Leaders**—for organizations of all kinds that want to build their leadership bench and empower their leaders for greater success
- **Coaching for World-Class Performance**—for companies that want to create a culture of world-class performance and world-class teamwork.

Jeff and his wife, Lori, make their home in Conway, Arkansas.

To learn more about Dr. Standridge or Jeff Standridge Innovation Partners, visit his website at JeffStandridge.com.